AFTERNOON TEA

AFTERNOON TEA

70 RECIPES FOR CAKES, BISCUITS AND PASTRIES,
ILLUSTRATED WITH 270 PHOTOGRAPHS

ANTONY WILD & SIMONA HILL

HERMES HOUSE

This edition is published by Hermes House
an imprint of Anness Publishing Ltd
Hermes House
88–89 Blackfriars Road
London SE1 8HA
tel. 020 7401 2077; fax 020 7633 9499

www.hermeshouse.com; www.annesspublishing.com

If you like the images in this book and would like
to investigate using them for publishing, promotions
or advertising, please visit our website
www.practicalpictures.com for more information.

Publisher: Joanna Lorenz
Editorial Director: Helen Sudell
Editor: Zoë Hughes Gough and Simona Hill
Photographer: Charlie Richards
Stylist: Liz Hippisley
Home Economist: Lucy Jessop
Designer: Simon Daley
Editorial Reader: Penelope Goodare
Production Controller: Mai Ling Collyer

ETHICAL TRADING POLICY

Because of our ongoing ecological investment programme,
you, as our customer, can have the pleasure and reassurance
of knowing that a tree is being cultivated on your behalf to
naturally replace the materials used to make the book you
are holding. For further information about this scheme, go to
www.annesspublishing.com/trees

COOK'S NOTES

- Bracketed terms are intended for American readers.
- For all recipes, quantities are given in both metric and imperial measures and, where appropriate, in standard cups and spoons. Follow one set, but not a mixture, because they are not interchangeable.
- Standard spoon and cup measures are level. 1 tsp = 5ml, 1 tbsp = 15ml, 1 cup = 250ml/8fl oz.
- Australian standard tablespoons are 20ml. Australian readers should use 3 tsp in place of 1 tbsp for measuring small quantities.
- The nutritional analysis given for each recipe is calculated per portion (i.e. serving or item), unless otherwise stated. If the recipe gives a range, such as Serves 4–6, then the nutritional analysis will be for the smaller portion size, i.e. 6 servings. Measurements for sodium do not include salt added to taste.
- Medium (US large) eggs are used unless otherwise stated.

PUBLISHER'S NOTE

ACKNOWLEDGEMENTS

Thanks to the following contributors:

Text for pages 6–9 and 12–21 written by Antony Wild.

Additional photographers: Martin Brigdale, Nicki Dowey,
Michelle Garrett, Amanda Heywood, William Lingwood,
Thomas Odulate, Craig Robertson.

Recipe writers: Pepita Aris, Catherine Atkinson, Alex Barker,
Michelle Berriedale Johnson, Kathy Brown, Maxine Clark,
Nicola Graimes, Maggie Mayhew, Anna Mossesson,
Christopher Trotter, Kate Whiteman, Biddy White Lennon,
Carol Wilson, Annette Yates.

Contents

Introduction

In 1615 the first use of a word relating to tea is recorded in the English language, when an East India Company associate in Japan, Mr Wickham, writes to his friend Mr Eaton asking him to buy a "pot of the best sort of chaw in Meaco", the place where the tea was grown for the Shogun, the chief military commander. It took a Portuguese princess, however, to introduce the British to the pleasures of drinking tea. In the summer of 1662 Catherine of Braganza arrived in England to become the bride of King Charles II. On landing at Portsmouth, the first thing she did was to ask for a cup of tea, taking the welcoming party completely by surprise (they had been preparing to serve her a glass of weak ale). Luckily a potential diplomatic crisis was averted by a retainer in her entourage who was able to produce the tea, and so the English Court was introduced to an old custom of the Portuguese nobility. Portugal's long trading association with China and Japan had made the Portuguese accustomed to what was still, at the time, a novelty in England, and certainly one that the Court had previously looked upon with some suspicion.

Catherine's endorsement of tea meant that the unfamiliar beverage suddenly became all the rage in London society – music to the ears of the directors of the East India Company. Founded by Royal Charter in 1600, the Company had been created to compete with the success of the Portuguese in capturing the hugely valuable spice trade from the East. But the Company had failed to dislodge its rivals, and its fortunes had fluctuated wildly. Its traders were aware of the existence of tea but at the time, the English were reluctant to take up tea-drinking as a habit. Tea was to be found on sale at some of London's coffee houses, albeit in a medicinal role, but it was not until the arrival of Catherine in England that the habit of drinking tea became established.

Tea becomes the English drink of choice

As tea-drinking spread, the East India Company directors realised the popularity of the product. A Mrs Harris was hired to serve the drink at all the Company meetings in the fine silver teapot presented to his fellow directors by Lord Berkeley in 1670. Two of the hallowed traditions of English business – the tea-lady and the tea-break – therefore owed their genesis, appropriately enough, to the Company that first imported tea.

By the middle of the 17th century, tea was in its ascendancy, with everyone from peasant farmer to the highest nobility in the land regularly drinking the beverage. Beer, the traditional drink of the working classes, was less popular, and so was coffee in the coffee houses – but tea triumphed behind the drawing room doors of the middle classes, demanding to be served. This Portuguese habit had taken the English by storm, although it was modified to reflect the unique character of the English. Fabulous outdoor tea gardens flourished at Vauxhall, Ranelagh Gardens and elsewhere in London. Here the fashionable set could see and be seen, and be entertained all the while as they took tea. Porcelain pots (their design adapted from Chinese wine jugs) were imported to brew the beverage in, and milk and sugar were added to the mix. The directors of the East India Company, which had the monopoly on the trade with China, rubbed their hands with glee: tea had become the single most valuable item of their trade.

The rise and fall of 'afternoon tea'

Tea was firmly established as the drink of choice, but the invention of 'afternoon tea', now seen as the quintessential English custom, did not occur until the 19th century. Although the innovation is usually attributed to a stroke of genius on the part of the 7th Countess of Bedford, in

Left The famous tea clipper, the Cutty Sark, *was designed to be the fastest of its kind in the world. Her maiden voyage was made to China in early 1870, and she returned later that year with the first of eight cargoes of almost 1500 tonnes of tea. This method of transporting tea was later superseded by steamships, which were more suited to navigating the newly built Panama Canal.*

*Above **Taking tea with friends has always been a valued social ritual.***

fact, the new habit was the result of the complex series of social and economic changes wrought over time by industrialization. Luncheon had been invented to fill the gap between breakfast and dinner, but this was a light meal. The evening meal of dinner was now served later than at any other time, and so a light snack in the afternoon became the way to stave off hunger. The custom of taking afternoon tea quickly became one of the defining rituals of English social life, giving rise to all manner of fashionable china and silver tea services as well as appetizing new snacks to accompany it. Many of the scenes in Oscar Wilde's most enduring play, *The Importance of Being Earnest* (1895), revolve around the afternoon tea table, its cakes and cucumber sandwiches, and when accused by a friend of eating too much, Algernon is able to respond with complete assurance, "I believe it is customary in good society to take some slight refreshment at five o'clock."

Initially a purely domestic phenomenon, by the end of the 19th century the serving of afternoon tea had been adopted by the large hotels which were springing up all over Britain – and in far-flung reaches of the British Empire. Elegant cafés followed suit, and even when silver cake stands and cucumber sandwiches were no longer to be found in homes, they could still be found

there. The tradition continued widely until the 1970s. After that date cafés increasingly became self-service. Working practices changed for most people and with them came new social habits. Only a few bastions of the old tradition remained – mainly the grand hotels and the occasional little teashop in a quaint rural town, with gingham tablecloths and homemade cakes.

A renaissance for afternoon tea

In the 1990s an increasing interest in quality teas conspired against the all-pervasive buzzing coffee bar boom, to remind people that there was a way of eating socially in an unhurried, elegant manner and in a way that appealed to people's sense of nostalgia. Afternoon tea returned to the national consciousness. While tea leaves remain an imported commodity, afternoon tea lends itself perfectly to the increasing trend towards the use of locally-sourced ingredients in homemade delicacies. In hotels, department stores and cafés across Britain, the public ritual of afternoon tea is once again enacted for the pleasure of thousands every day.

Although the fashionable private salons for taking afternoon tea in the style of the Countess of Bedford may no longer be found, the tradition of afternoon tea is maintained, but as a treat rather than on a daily basis. An enormous variety of teas have become available now, and keen cooks can exert their talents over a range of traditional and newly created delicacies.

The afternoon tea table

The new 19th-century phenomenon of afternoon tea was not only good for tea importers, it heralded a growth in several attendant industries, such as the production of fine china and porcelain tea services and the manufacture of silverware.

The East India Company made huge profits out of the tea that they brought from China, and so did the government, who applied hefty taxes to the product. To increase sales, the importers quickly realized that their new customers needed something to brew the tea in. The Chinese were used to brewing tea in powdered form in a tea cup, but towards the end of the 14th century larger leaved teas had become popular, requiring a brewing vessel, and the Chinese, who had made growing and brewing tea a skill akin to that of wine production, had adapted their traditional wine pots to this purpose, adding a handle and a spout.

The first appearance of the teapot

This appealing Chinese design found favour with the English when they became interested in drinking tea, and many stoneware pots of this kind were exported back to England. These in turn spawned imitators, principally in

Staffordshire, and the familiar 'Brown Betty' teapot evolved, a utilitarian vessel, with a high sheen glaze, reputed to make the best pot of tea. While not the most elegant of teapots, it has the virtue of durability – and given the sheer quantity of tea being brewed in Britain at the time, that was not to be underestimated. Like the teapot itself, the design has stood the test of time and can still be seen in many households to this day.

Fine china

Such workaday items as the Brown Betty teapot, however, were not suited to the elegant style of service that tea drinking demanded among the fashionable, well-heeled set. Consequently, it was Chinese porcelain which lent the most lustre to the new custom in Britain. This was the era of the craze for 'Chinoiserie', when Chinese silks, wallpapers, screens and porcelain were the must-have items for any distinguished household.

Below The fine tradition of taking afternoon tea necessitated an equally elegant tea service in which to present it.

Below Industrialization meant that pottery was widely available to everyone to purchase at reasonable cost.

Above Every fashionable house, teashop or hotel tearoom possessed an attractive fine china tea service, as porcelain became the material of choice for making and serving tea.

The Company's merchants started to exploit these markets, eventually involving themselves in the design and production process in China. Many a noble house in the 18th century would display dinner services of fine porcelain emblazoned with their coats of arms, hand-painted on the other side of the world. Teapots, teacups and saucers were now added to the shopping list among a growing range of other tea-serving items.

The Chinese dominance of the porcelain industry, could not last however. German alchemists discovered the formula for making porcelain, and later Josiah Wedgwood of England was credited with industrializing the production of pottery on a scale never seen before. It was not long before other manufacturers followed suit. Elements of Chinese designs such as the ubiquitous 'Willow Pattern', 'Blanc de Chine' and others were shamelessly plundered, and remain popular even now.

It was not just the demand for teapots that fuelled the porcelain boom. During the 18th century British tea drinkers discovered a taste for black teas (as opposed to the green teas they had drunk initially) and found that these bitter teas worked particularly well with the addition of milk and sugar. This was good news for dairy farmers, West Indian sugar planters and porcelain manufacturers, who produced suitable vessels for the new additions. Then, in the last century, along came the idea of afternoon tea with its cakes and sandwiches, and yet more items were required to make up a tea service.

Silverware and linen

Alongside the East India Company – who retained their monopoly on the tea trade with China until 1834 – and porcelain manufacturers, others benefited commercially from the fashion for tea. Silver manufacturers were required to create sugar tongs, strainers, teaspoons, cake stands and small cutlery to enhance the daintiness of the offering, as well as teapots, milk jugs and sugar bowls for the top-notch tearooms. Linen mills, embroiderers and lacemakers did well likewise in producing tablecloths and napkins – even the innovation of the humble doily was a spin-off from the unstoppable growth in demand for tea.

But the teapot always was and remains the undisputed star of the proceedings. Over the years endless sleek styling and technical innovation in design has been dedicated to the teapot over its illustrious career. What makes it all the more curious, in Britain at least, is that the conservative, ever-reliable earthenware teapot remains the default teapot of choice in many households – and for that we have to thank an anonymous 14th-century Chinese craftsman.

The etiquette of afternoon tea

Over two centuries of tradition have led to a wealth of customs and codes of behaviour that must be followed if you wish to display proper tea-time manners in genteel society. Smart clothes and good manners are always welcomed at the tea table.

When serving afternoon tea the hostess should bring all the essential items to the tea table on a large tray. The tray should be set down on the table and the individual items arranged appropriately. Platters of sandwiches and cake stands should be placed in the middle of the table and the teapot should be positioned with the spout facing the hostess, or pourer. In front of each guest a teacup should be placed on a saucer with a teaspoon resting on the right side, a small plate with a fork for eating cake (or knife if you are serving anything that requires spreading) and a napkin. The milk jug and sugar bowl should be arranged near the centre.

Pouring the tea perfectly

A warm teapot should be filled immediately when the water boils, and be brought to the table on a tray where it can stand while the tea brews. When the tea is ready

to pour, the pourer should take the teapot to each guest and pour carefully into each cup. Tea is traditionally served in a cup holding 120ml/4fl oz of liquid and should be three-quarters filled with tea. The size is not imperative, but a teacup should be shallower and wider than a coffee cup to allow the tea to cool slightly before drinking.

Demure tea drinking

Once the tea has been poured, guests may add milk or lemon (offered in delicate slices) and sugar. It is preferable to use gentle to-and-fro movements with the teaspoon rather than wide, noisy circular motions. The spoon should then be placed on the saucer to rest.

If seated at the table, the correct etiquette is to lift the teacup only to drink the tea and replace it on the saucer between sips. If there is no table, the saucer should be held in the left hand on your lap and the teacup in your

Below If scones are served at tea, split in half, butter, then top with jam and finish with a dollop of clotted cream.

Below Sandwiches should always be served in delicate fingers, triangles or squares, to enable graceful eating.

Above A properly arranged tea tray is loaded with a teapot, a cake stand, cake knife, teacups and saucers, side plates, napkins, forks, teaspoons, sugar bowl and milk jug.

right hand. It should be returned to the saucer when not in use. The cup should be held daintily by the handle between the thumb and fingers, with the little finger extended for balance. Never hold the teacup in the palm of your hand or loop your fingers through the handle. And by no means wave the cup around.

Tea should be drunk in small, silent sips from the cup with as much grace and elegance as possible.

Elegant eating

The correct size of plate to use for serving sandwiches, cakes, pastries and other delicacies at afternoon tea is between 15 and 20cm (6 and 8in). The hostess must ensure that guests are provided with the necessary cutlery for the food that is served. It is customary to serve wafer-thin sandwiches cut into dainty triangles

and with crusts removed. Finger food can also be served. A slice of cake, scones with jam and cream, or a selection of biscuits are appropriate to serve.

When enjoying afternoon tea at a table, place the napkin on your lap and, if you leave the table temporarily for any reason, set the napkin on the seat.

All food should be eaten in delicate bites, with the utmost attention to detail. Think about how you will appear to your fellow guests at the tea table. When not in use forks should be rested on the side of the plate with the tines down. Never place them back on the table once they have been used. Similarly, place used knives on the side of the plate.

A social event

Above all, afternoon tea is a sociable occasion to be enjoyed with friends and family. So remember to smile and make polite conversation (between mouthfuls, of course) and savour this most quintessential of English afternoon traditions.

A perfect pot of tea

Whether your preference is for green, black, herbal or flavoured, there is nothing more refreshing in the afternoon than a pot of freshly brewed tea. Aficionados have maxims of their own on what constitutes the perfect cup of tea, and many blends are mentioned here, but they all agree that utmost care should be taken in making it. Step-by-step instructions for brewing are given. If you prefer a cool drink on a hot day, or you wish to offer a choice, there are also some suggestions for alternative drinks to serve at the 'tea table'.

Teas of the world

There are a bewildering number of teas, with quality ranging from the fabled imperial 'monkey-picked' tea of China, so called because it was collected from inaccessible locations, to the rare Ceylon 'Silver Tips', and from 'speciality' blends like Earl Grey to machine-harvested, blended black teas.

India, China and Sri Lanka dominate the tea-producing world. Together India and China produce more than half of all tea consumed. India produces enormous amounts of tea – its 14,000 plantations employ one million people. Kenya, Turkey, Indonesia and Malawi are also tea producers. Teas sold purely by their particular country or region of origin for example, those from India and Sri Lanka, are known as speciality teas.

Speciality teas

These are the aristocrats of the tea world and are considered sufficiently refined and distinctive to be drunk unblended. India and Sri Lanka produce speciality teas as well as

Below Ceylon tea is a black tea, with citrus notes to the flavour, grown on the island of Sri Lanka (formerly Ceylon).

blended teas from plantations in distinct regions. India is best known for its delicate Darjeelings and robust Assams. Assam is also known as British tea because of the British inclination to take strong-flavoured tea with milk and sugar.

The region of Darjeeling produces the 'champagne of teas', prized for its light colour and fine flavour. The

Left India has three tea-producing regions – Darjeeling, Assam and Nilgiri – and a blend of teas from these plantations produces Indian tea.

first crop of the year is known as the 'first flush' and has a fanatical following in northern Germany. Darjeelings are all grown for export.

Assam, the other leading Indian tea, comes from the valley of the lower Brahmaputra River where indigenous tea plants were discovered in the 1840s. The Assam Company, which still exists today, pioneered the estate system there. The best Assams have a rich, almost tarry flavour. Lesser ones are often used to give strength to blends such as English Breakfast.

In Sri Lanka too, teas are often packaged according to the plantation or tea garden from which they are hand picked. The government of that country still permits the use of the old colonial name of Ceylon in

Below Assam tea, manufactured from leaves picked in the Assam region of India, has a full-bodied flavour.

Right In a tea plantation in Assam, India, workers pluck 'two leaves and a bud' by hand in the traditional way. The leaves at the tip are younger and finer than the rest of the bush.

connection with its fine, golden teas. The two best known are the pungent Uvas of the east and softer Dimbulas of the west. China, like India and Sri Lanka, produces many speciality teas.

Tea blends

A blend is a mixture of leaves from different plantations. Blends occur in India as well as other countries, though, like olive oil and wine, blended tea is not for the purist. Some blends are machine-harvested teas and all play an undistinguished role in the proprietary mixtures of tea that are widely sold.

A few anomalies exist however, defined as speciality tea, but created from a blend, none more so than the blend known as Earl Grey, the best selling speciality tea of all. This blend of black teas is flavoured with essence of bergamot, and tea companies frequently claim to have some unique access to the original

recipe. However, Earl Grey, the popular British Prime Minister who saw the Reform Act through Parliament in the 1830s, almost certainly had nothing to do with its formulation. Although the blend is supposedly of Chinese origin, in fact the bergamot fruit is a spontaneous mutation of the bitter orange, and has never been grown in China.

Earl Grey tea is best enjoyed black, or with a splash of milk, or a slice of lemon.

Another blend which has speciality tea status is 'English Breakfast' (also known as 'Irish' and "Royal Breakfast') which could consist of teas from anywhere, the only consensus being that they should be of a reasonably high quality and have a strong flavour.

Below Darjeeling tea, named after the Darjeeling region of West Bengal in India, has a unique much sought-after muscatel flavour.

Below Earl Grey tea is infused with bergamot, the pungent oil of a citrus fruit. It is one of the most popular 'speciality' teas in Britain and North America.

Below English breakfast tea is a blended tea with a strong flavour intended to be offset by the addition of milk and sugar.

Right Jasmine tea is a green tea or black China tea with added jasmine petals, which are valued for their delicate floral flavour.

Picking tea

Tea is picked from the plant *Camellia sinensis*, which is a hardy bush, not unlike the common privet hedge, and is kept to a height of about 1.2m (4ft) on tea plantations. The quality and taste of tea are affected by many factors including the time of year that the tea is picked, the way it is picked, the climate of the region where the plantation is situated, the altitude and direction that the plantation faces, as well as the quality of the soil. Consecutive years may produce completely different qualities of crop from the same plantation.

The tea plants are dormant through the winter, turning green in spring. The youngest 'two leaves and a bud' are handpicked from the bush in early spring, and then sometimes up to two or three times a week at peak harvest times. The first tips picked in spring have

collected the most essential oil and for this reason are known as 'golden tips' – the most expensive picking.

Tea manufacturing

Broadly speaking, there are three principal methods of treating tea leaves and all are carried out on or near the tea plantation. Leaves can

be immediately 'fired', that is, quickly heated in a metal pan to dry them out, the leaves being gently rolled at the same time. This method produces green tea, the backbone of the China tea industry.

The second method involves 'withering' (a gentle initial drying), and then the leaves are cut and torn by machines opening their cell structure up to oxidation, or 'fermentation' as the industry calls it. The blackened fragments of the tea leaves are then dried further in their final stage of production, and finally graded by size. 'Orange Pekoe' and 'Broken Orange Pekoe' are the two largest sizes remaining, the smallest being 'Fannings' and 'Dust'. These sizes of leaf are black teas, which form about 90 per cent of the world's production today.

Halfway between green and black teas is 'Oolong', a semi-fermented tea mainly produced in China and Taiwan, and much prized by connoisseurs for its peachy flavour. Oolong is often referred to as a blue-green tea because of the colour of the leaves of the plant.

Below Green tea is becoming the drink of choice for those concerned with improving their health.

Below White tea, with its delicate, sweet flavour, is made from very young, tender leaves that are quickly fired.

Right Oolong tea is halfway between green and black tea in appearance and flavour. The best have a hint of peaches in the taste.

To the main varieties of green, black and Oolong teas must be added other variations. The most well known of these are Lapsang Souchong, a Chinese black tea which has been smoked over a fire of spruce, and jasmine tea, a green or black China tea blended with Jasmine petals.

Black teas

The black teas that dominate today were initially developed by the British on new plantations in Sri Lanka and India. Not wishing to emulate the extremely labour-intensive production methods of China, the British pioneered the idea of using machinery to speed the process up and bring the price down. Black teas were effectively the first industrialized teas, and enjoyed great worldwide commercial success. As a result the tea-producing colonies that made up the British empire started consuming teas in vast quantities too. Today India, the world's largest producer, has to import tea in order to feed the habit they acquired from the British. The British tea 'estate' system was successfully exported to Britain's East African colonies, with the result that some of the finest blending teas in the world now come from Malawi and Kenya. Their bright orangey flavour makes these teas a brisk, refreshing brew.

Green teas

Almost all green teas originate in China – where tea has been produced for more than 2,000 years – and Japan, where a Buddhist monk introduced it in the 9th century and where it became

central to Japan's famous tea ceremonies. In fact, 80 per cent of the tea that China produces is green tea, the daily drink of the Chinese people. Green tea was widely drunk in Europe before black tea became more popular. The health benefits of green tea in protecting against heart disease and certain types of cancer have been widely recognized of late, and it is now better known in the West than it used to be. Specialists can now be found dealing only in green tea. The most common of the Chinese green teas is 'Gunpowder'. In this variety the leaves are tightly rolled into pellets. The astringent 'Sencha' is the best known of the Japanese tea varieties.

White teas

This little known tea variety comes from the same plant as green tea, black tea and Oolong tea, but it is uncured and unoxidized. The fresh leaves have a white downy coat. Once picked, they are fast-dried rather than roasted. White tea comprises buds and young leaves, which have been found to contain

less caffeine than older leaves. White teas are thought to be the most beneficial to health, since they contain greater numbers of antioxidants, which are known to help fight cancers. However, this tea needs brewing for a long time in order for the flavour to be released.

Below Lapsang Souchong, a Chinese tea, has a smoky flavour derived from drying the tea leaves over spruce fires.

Herbal and flavoured teas

The average cup of tea contains about half the amount of caffeine of an equivalent cup of coffee. Many people, however, are concerned about consuming excessive quantities of the caffeine. For them, herb and fruit teas, or tisanes, are the ideal substitute.

Herbal and fruit teas frequently, but not always, contain no 'real' tea (derived from the bush *Camellia sinensis*). The case against caffeine has led to an enormous surge in demand for herbal and fruit teas. Many of these tisanes offer a range of delights for the palate, and some herb teas may have genuine medicinal properties. The key issue in this respect is the level of essential oils left in the plant material used in the blends.

An anomaly exists here too: 'Moroccan mint' sounds as if it should be pure mint, but in fact is mint blended with black tea. The result of this proliferation is that the grocer's shelf is a minefield for those wanting to drink 'healthy', caffeinate-free tea. Reading the packet carefully is the only solution.

Herbal teas

The essential oils in all herb teas decay with oxidation and time, so the best way to reap the benefits is to buy them fresh, or preserved in sachets. Depending on where you live, some herb teas can be grown in your garden or window box, and there is something particularly pleasing about drinking a preparation of the leaves of a plant that you have grown yourself.

Chamomile tea is traditionally associated with inducing sleep and a calmed state – making a fresh brew with leaves just picked ensures the essential oils go into the brew. Other popular herb teas include

Below Ginger tea is made using slices of the ginger root, which can be bought in supermarkets and health stores.

Above Chamomile tea can be made using fresh or dried flowers.

peppermint and fennel, which act as aids to digestion, lime flower, nettle and verbena. Tea manufacturers have made considerable efforts over the last few years to create blends claiming specific effects. Teas with names like 'Tranquillity', 'Yogi' and 'Detox' are available, but check the essential oil content before you buy.

Below Mint tea is easy to make, using the fresh herb peppermint. Pick a sprig and infuse in boiling water.

Above Ginseng tea is said to have many health benefits. The tea is made from the fleshy root.

Fruit teas

The packets of fruit blends claim no such medicinal effects, and are drunk purely for their flavour, which like any new tea, is an acquired taste. However, it is possible to buy fruit teas that use purely natural ingredients, as opposed to artificial or 'nature identical', meaning created in a laboratory to replicate the flavour it purports to be. Such fruit flavours may well be tasty, but they have never had the benefit of sunshine or a warm breeze.

Beware though, many fruit teas have black tea as a base and are

Below Naturally caffeine free, Rooibos is derived from the plant of that name.

flavoured with the fruit zest or dried fruit as part of the manufacturing process. Lemon tea, made by adding lemon slices to black tea, may well be the precursor of fruit teas. Always read the label carefully.

Below Nettle tea is made from the young leaves of stinging nettles. Its flavour is unlike any other.

Above Fruit teas can be caffeine-free infusions of dehydrated fruits.

A healthy balance

Many tea drinkers regard herb and fruit teas with suspicion, but these infusions are becoming increasingly popular as the health issues surrounding caffeine consumption become more widely recognized.

The art of brewing tea

The key ingredient of a perfect cup of tea is easily taken for granted – it is none other than water. This should be freshly drawn, which means that the cold tap should be allowed to run for half a minute, at least, before the kettle is filled.

Water that has been sitting in the pipes overnight is stale and flat. Likewise twice-boiled water is dull and lifeless, so empty the kettle before filling it with fresh. The hardness of your water supply has a great influence on the quality of your tea. Some manufacturers even go to the lengths of making specific blends for specific areas. Very soft water mutes the nuances of flavour in a tea, and very hard water tends to dull the appearance of the brew and can create an unpleasant scum. Filtering the water before boiling always improves its performance.

1 Always warm the pot before measuring in the tea. Either hold the inverted pot over the spout of the kettle as it boils, or swill the teapot with boiling water before adding the tea leaves.

2 There is no fixed amount of tea that one should use – the old adage of 'one spoon per person and one for the pot' is a vague guide. Large leaf teas occupy more volume than small leafed ones, and the measure should be adjusted accordingly.

3 Tea brews best at boiling point, so pour the water on to the tea leaves as soon as the water boils. Stir briskly. Allow to stand for at least 3 minutes before pouring.

4 Pour the tea through a tea strainer.

Adding lemon: Many people drink black tea with a slice of lemon for added zest – something that makes the tea purists shudder. Never add milk to tea that is flavoured with lemon.

Adding milk: To temper the bitterness of black tea, milk can be added. When everyone drank the same blends of tea, old-fashioned polite protocol used to require that milk be poured into the cup before the tea. There are so many varieties of tea on offer these days that the tradition doesn't seem so appropriate.

Adding sugar: As with the addition of lemon, sweetness is all a matter of individual preference. White sugar can be added to black tea, tea with milk and lemon tea.

Making tea with fresh herbs

The same general rules apply for brewing herbal infusions from fresh leaves as they do for brewing tea from dried leaves. The exception is fresh ginger tea made using thin slices of peeled root ginger: this should be allowed to steep for at least 5 minutes.

1 The difference here with making tea is that you need to pick your own leaves, so correct plant identification is crucial. Use a sprig of your chosen herb per person.

2 Either add the herb to the warmed teapot or, if you are making an individual cup, you could put the sprig straight into the cup. Remember, the leaves will remain visible.

3 Pour on boiling water and allow the herb to steep. When it has reached the desired strength, strain the liquid into the cup, if you used a teapot, and enjoy.

Cold drinks for hot summer days

Homemade, thirst-quenching soft drinks, freshly made with quality ingredients, are enjoyable to make and taste nothing like the manufactured sugary drinks that are sold commercially. These are deliciously refreshing on hot summer days.

Still lemonade

Fresh lemonade has been a traditional drink for many generations. Nowadays it is often seen on the menu in smart contemporary cafés and teashops.

SERVES 4–6
3 unwaxed lemons
115g/4oz/generous ½ cup caster (superfine) sugar

1 Pare the skin from the lemons with a vegetable peeler. Put the lemon rind and sugar into a bowl, add 900ml/1½ pints/3¾ cups boiling water and stir well until the sugar dissolves.

2 Cover and leave to cool. Squeeze the juice from the lemons. Add it to the flavoured water, mix well and strain into a jug (pitcher). Chill and serve in tall glasses with ice.

Energy 115kcal/489kJ; Protein 0.2g; Carbohydrate 30.4g, of which sugars 30.4g; Fat 0g, of which saturates 0g; Cholesterol 0mg; Calcium 17mg; Fibre 0g; Sodium 2mg.

Barley water

Like lemonade, barley water is an old-fashioned drink. It is usually served cold, but is equally delicious as a hot drink.

SERVES 10, TO DILUTE
50g/2oz/⅓ cup pearl barley, washed
rind and juice of 1 lemon
caster (superfine) sugar, to taste
mineral water, to serve

1 In a large pan cover the pearl barley with cold water. Bring to the boil and simmer gently for 2 minutes. Strain the liquid. Return the barley to the rinsed pan.

2 Add the lemon rind and 600ml/1 pint/2½ cups water to the barley. Bring to the boil over a medium heat and simmer gently for 1½–2 hours, stirring occasionally.

3 Strain the liquid into a jug (pitcher), add the lemon juice, and sweeten to taste. Leave to cool. Dilute to taste.

Energy 38kcal/161kJ; Protein 0.4g; Carbohydrate 9.4g, of which sugars 5.3g; Fat 0g, of which saturates 0g; Cholesterol 3.8mg; Calcium 21mg; Fibre 0g; Sodium 0.5mg.

Fresh orange squash

Pushing oranges through a juicer rather than squeezing out the juice means you maximize the fruits' goodness and reduce the amount of wastage.

MAKES 550ML/18FL OZ/2½ CUPS, TO DILUTE
90g/3½oz/½ cup caster (superfine) sugar
6 large oranges
still or sparkling mineral water, to serve

1 Put the sugar in a small, heavy pan with 100ml/ 3½fl oz/scant ½ cup water. Heat gently, stirring until the sugar has dissolved. Bring to the boil and boil rapidly for 3 minutes until the mixture is syrupy. Remove from the heat and leave to cool.

2 Using a parer, or sharp knife, cut away the skins from three of the six oranges. Chop the flesh into pieces small enough to fit through the funnel of a juicer.

3 Chop the remaining oranges, with skins on, into similar-size pieces.

4 Push all the orange pieces through the juicer, then mix with the sugar syrup. Pour into a bottle or jug (pitcher) and store in the refrigerator. To serve, dilute the orange squash to taste with still or sparkling mineral water.

Energy 725kcal/3093kJ; Protein 11.4g; Carbohydrate 179.1g, of which sugars 179.1g; Fat 1g, of which saturates 0g; Cholesterol 0mg; Calcium 518mg; Fibre 17g; Sodium 55mg.

Ruby red berry squash

This intensely coloured, fruity-flavoured drink uses blackberries or blueberries, or a mixture of the two, to make a sweet but refreshing fruit squash.

MAKES 350ML/12FL OZ/1½ CUPS, TO DILUTE
350g/12oz/3 cups blackberries or blueberries
130g/4 ½oz/scant ¾ cup golden caster
   (superfine) sugar
sparkling mineral water, to serve

1 Remove any tough stalks or leaves from the fruit. Wash the fruit thoroughly and allow to dry.

2 Push handfuls of the fruit through a juicer.

3 Put the sugar in a small, heavy pan with 100ml/ 3½fl oz/scant ½ cup water. Heat gently until the sugar dissolves, stirring with a wooden spoon, then bring to the boil and boil for 3 minutes until syrupy. Leave until completely cool.

4 Mix the fruit juice with the syrup in a jug (pitcher). Chill in the refrigerator. For each serving pour about 50ml/2fl oz/¼ cup fruit syrup into a glass.

5 Add ice and top up with sparkling mineral water.

Energy 712kcal/3020kJ; Protein 4.2g; Carbohydrate 184.8g, of which sugars 170.8g; Fat 0g, of which saturates 0g; Cholesterol 0mg; Calcium 69mg; Fibre 7g; Sodium 8mg.

Savoury treats

Traditionally, afternoon tea begins with a savoury course. A delectable selection of dainty sandwiches, thinly sliced with crusts removed, tempts the tastebuds and whets the appetite. Served alongside these for a more substantial between-meals filler are rich flaky pastry quiches, homemade sausage rolls, crisp crackers and light and flavourful spreads.

Sandwiches

The classic afternoon tea commences with a round of dainty sandwiches, which can be elegantly nibbled while you sip your first cup of freshly brewed tea. The sandwiches can be made of brown or white bread, but should always be cut into small fingers, triangles or squares.

Cucumber sandwiches

Delicate cucumber sandwiches with crusts removed are synonymous with traditional afternoon tea.

SERVES 6

1 cucumber
12 slices white bread
butter, at room temperature, for spreading
salt and ground black pepper

1 Peel the cucumber and cut into thin slices. Sprinkle with salt and put in a colander to drain for 20 minutes.

2 Butter the bread on one side. Trim off the crusts. Arrange the cucumber over six slices of bread and sprinkle with pepper. Top with the remaining bread. Press down lightly.

3 Cut the sandwiches into fingers, squares or triangles. Arrange on a serving plate.

Energy 174kcal/735kJ; Protein 6.8g; Carbohydrate 29.2g, of which sugars 3.3g; Fat 4.2g, of which saturates 1.1g; Cholesterol 5mg; Calcium 92mg; Fibre 1g; Sodium 307mg.

Turkey and cranberry sandwiches

Perfect for the festive season, turkey and cranberry sandwiches taste delicious and distinctly moreish.

SERVES 6

12 slices wholemeal (whole-wheat) bread
butter, at room temperature, for spreading
300g/12oz roast turkey, sliced
90ml/6 tbsp cranberry sauce

1 Spread each slice of bread with butter. Cover half of the slices of bread with roast turkey.

2 Spoon 15ml/1 tbsp of cranberry sauce on to the turkey and spread out to the edges. Season with salt and pepper. Top with another slice of bread and press down lightly.

3 Cut each sandwich into quarters diagonally to make small triangles.

Energy 312kcal/1314kJ; Protein 20g; Carbohydrate 35.4g, of which sugars 11.5g; Fat 11.3g, of which saturates 6.2g; Cholesterol 63mg; Calcium 40mg; Fibre 3.5g; Sodium 435mg.

Egg and cress sandwiches

A well-made egg and mayonnaise sandwich is a tasty tea-time snack.

SERVES 6

12 thin slices white or brown bread
butter, at room temperature, for
   spreading
4 small (US medium) hard-boiled
   eggs, peeled and finely chopped
60ml/4 tbsp mayonnaise
1 carton mustard and cress (fine
   curled cress)
salt and ground black pepper
slices of lemon, to garnish

1 Trim the crusts off the bread,
using a sharp knife. Then spread the
slices with soft butter.

2 To make the filling, put the
chopped eggs, mayonnaise,
mustard and cress and seasoning in
a bowl and mix.

3 Spoon on to six slices of bread
and spread out to the edges. Top
each one with another slice of bread
and press down gently. Cut into neat
triangles. Garnish with lemon slices.

COOK'S TIP
These sandwiches will keep well
for 2–3 hours. Cover with damp
kitchen paper, then cover tightly
in clear film (plastic wrap). Chill.

Egg and tuna sandwiches

*A flavourful and popular combination,
tuna fish and egg sandwiches are
perfect at any time of year.*

SERVES 6

12 thin slices white or brown bread
butter, at room temperature,
   for spreading
4 small (US medium) hard-boiled
   eggs, peeled and finely chopped
50g/2oz canned tuna fish in oil,
   drained and mashed
10ml/2 tsp paprika
squeeze of lemon juice
50g/2oz piece cucumber, peeled
   and thinly sliced
salt and ground black pepper

1 Trim the crusts off the bread, then
spread with butter.

2 To make the filling, mix the eggs
with the tuna, paprika, lemon juice
and seasoning.

3 Cover six slices of bread with the
cucumber, top with the tuna and
finish with another slice of bread.
Cut each sandwich into three fingers.

Egg and cress Energy 320kcal/1337kJ; Protein 9g; Carbohydrate 26.8g, of which sugars 1.6g; Fat 20.5g, of which saturates 7.8g; Cholesterol 157mg; Calcium 89mg; Fibre 0.9g; Sodium 450mg.
Egg and tuna Energy 273kcal/1145kJ; Protein 12.3g; Carbohydrate 25.7g, of which sugars 1.2g; Fat 14.6g, of which saturates 6.9g; Cholesterol 154mg; Calcium 58mg; Fibre 3.5g; Sodium 477mg.

Crab sandwiches

Bread and butter served with crab is a classic tea-time treat.

SERVES 6

3 cooked crabs, about 900g/2lb each
12 slices crusty wholegrain bread
butter, at room temperature, for spreading
2 lemons, cut into quarters
rocket (arugula)
salt and ground black pepper

1 Break off the crab claws and legs, then use your thumbs to ease the body out of the shell. Remove and discard the grey gills from the body and put the white meat in a bowl.

2 Scrape the brown meat from the shell and add to the white meat. Season with salt and pepper.

3 Butter the bread and spread the crab meat on half of the slices. Add a squeeze of lemon juice and a little rocket. Top with bread and cut into triangles.

Energy 526kcal/2209kJ; Protein 30.1g; Carbohydrate 56g, of which sugars 2.6g; Fat 21.7g, of which saturates 9.1g; Cholesterol 85mg; Calcium 117mg; Fibre 7.7g; Sodium 1150mg.

Cheese and pickle sandwiches

Sharp, mature cheese is complemented with tangy pickle.

SERVES 6

12 slices white bread, crusts removed
butter, at room temperature, for spreading
300g/12oz hard cheese, such as Cheddar
90ml/6 tbsp pickle
watercress or rocket (arugula), to garnish
salt and ground black pepper

1 Spread each slice of bread with butter. Thinly slice the cheese and arrange the slices over half of the slices, filling to the edges.

2 Spoon 15ml/1 tbsp of pickle on to the cheese and season with salt and pepper, to taste. Spread the pickle out to the edges. Top each one with another slice of bread.

3 Cut each sandwich into three equal portions. Arrange on a plate and garnish with watercress or rocket.

Energy 429kcal/1793kJ; Protein 17.4g; Carbohydrate 31.8g, of which sugars 6.4g; Fat 25.6g, of which saturates 16.5g; Cholesterol 72mg; Calcium 433mg; Fibre 1g; Sodium 972mg.

Roast beef and horseradish sandwiches

Piquant horseradish is a perfect accompaniment for beef.

SERVES 6

1 large crusty white loaf
butter, at room temperature, for spreading
300g/12oz roast beef, thinly sliced
30–60ml/2–4 tbsp horseradish sauce
rocket (arugula)
salt and ground black pepper

1 Using a sharp bread knife, generously cut 12 even slices from the loaf of white bread. Spread each with butter.

2 Allowing about 50g/2oz of beef per sandwich, top half of the slices with meat and horseradish sauce, to taste.

3 Add some rocket to each sandwich. Sprinkle with salt and black pepper. Top each one with another slice of bread, and cut each sandwich diagonally into quarters.

Energy 505kcal/2125kJ; Protein 27.3g; Carbohydrate 58.5g, of which sugars 3g; Fat 19.6g, of which saturates 11g; Cholesterol 79mg; Calcium 148mg; Fibre 1.6g; Sodium 838mg.

Ham and English mustard sandwiches

Cold ham sandwiches are an old-fashioned favourite.

SERVES 6

12 slices seeded bread
butter, at room temperature, for spreading
300g/12oz roast ham, thinly sliced
30–60ml/1–2 tbsp English (hot) mustard
salt and ground black pepper
4 tomatoes and ½ carton cress, to garnish

1 Trim the crusts from each slice of bread, then spread with butter. Top half with thin slices of roast ham, and add English mustard to taste, spreading to the edges.

2 Top each one with a slice of bread and press down gently. Then cut each sandwich into three equal portions. Cut the tomatoes into wedges and chop the cress.

3 Arrange the sandwiches on a plate and garnish with the tomato and cress.

Energy 275kcal/1157kJ; Protein 15.2g; Carbohydrate 28.8g, of which sugars 2.2g; Fat 11.9g, of which saturates 6.3g; Cholesterol 52mg; Calcium 55mg; Fibre 2.6g; Sodium 1171mg.

Potted cheese

This a great way to use up odd pieces of cheese left on the cheeseboard, blending them with your chosen seasonings and adjusting the flavour before adding alcohol. Garnish with parsley and serve with plain crackers, oatcakes or crisp toast.

SERVES 4–6

250g/9oz hard cheese, such as
  mature Cheddar or Stilton
75g/3oz/6 tbsp soft, unsalted
  butter, plus 25g/1oz/1 tbsp extra
  for melting
pinch of dried English (hot)
  mustard
pinch of ground mace
30ml/2 tbsp sherry or port
sprigs of fresh parsley,
  to garnish
ground black pepper

1 Cut the cheese into rough pieces and put them into the bowl of a food processor. Use the pulse button to chop the cheese into crumbs.

2 Add the butter, mustard, mace and pepper and blend until smooth. Taste and adjust the seasoning.

> **COOK'S TIP**
> Use finely chopped chives instead of mustard for a change.

3 Blend in the sherry or port.

4 Spoon the mixture into a dish leaving about 1cm/½in to spare on top. Level the surface.

5 Melt the butter in a small pan, skimming off any foam that rises to the surface. Leaving the sediment in the pan, pour a layer of melted butter on top of the cheese mixture to cover the surface. Refrigerate.

Energy 262kcal/1082kJ; Protein 10.7g; Carbohydrate 0.2g, of which sugars 0.2g; Fat 23.6g, of which saturates 15.2g; Cholesterol 70mg; Calcium 290mg; Fibre 0g; Sodium 363mg.

Salmon mousse

This light and delicate mousse is ideal for tea on the lawn on a balmy summer's afternoon. Garnish it with thinly sliced cucumber, delicious when in season, and lemon wedges. Serve with thin plain crackers or Melba toast for a satisfying crunch.

SERVES 6–8

300ml/½ pint/1¼ cups milk
1 small onion, thinly sliced
1 small carrot, thinly sliced
2 bay leaves
2 sprigs of parsley or dill
6 whole peppercorns
15ml/1 tbsp powdered gelatine
350g/12oz salmon fillet
75ml/5 tbsp dry white vermouth
25g/1oz/2 tbsp butter
25g/1oz/4 tbsp plain
   (all-purpose) flour
75ml/5 tbsp mayonnaise
150ml/¼ pint/⅔ cup whipping
   cream
salt and ground black pepper

1 Put the milk in a pan with half the onion, carrot, herbs and peppercorns. Bring slowly to the boil, remove from the heat, cover and leave to infuse for 30 minutes. Meanwhile, sprinkle the gelatine over 45ml/ 3 tbsp cold water and leave to soak.

2 Put the salmon in another pan with the remaining onion, carrot, herbs and peppercorns. Add the vermouth and 60ml/4 tbsp water. Simmer, covered, for 10 minutes.

3 Flake the fish into a bowl, discarding the skin and bones. Boil the juices in the pan to reduce by half, strain and reserve.

4 Strain the infused milk into a clean pan and add the butter and flour. Whisking continuously, cook until thickened, then simmer gently for 1 minute. Pour into a food processor, add the soaked gelatine and blend. Add the salmon and the reserved cooking juices and pulse briefly.

5 Put into a bowl and stir in the mayonnaise and seasonings. Whip the cream and fold in gently. Pour into an oiled mould, cover and refrigerate for about 2 hours.

Energy 285kcal/1183kJ; Protein 12.6g; Carbohydrate 5.8g, of which sugars 3.2g; Fat 22.7g, of which saturates 8.7g; Cholesterol 57mg; Calcium 73mg; Fibre 0.2g; Sodium 103mg.

Quiche Lorraine

This classic quiche has some delightful characteristics, namely very thin flaky pastry, a really creamy and light, egg-rich filling, and smoked bacon. It makes an indulgent and satisfying first course to an afternoon tea.

SERVES 4–6

175g/6oz/1½ cups plain (all-purpose) flour, sifted, plus extra for dusting
pinch of salt
1 egg yolk
115g/4oz/½ cup unsalted butter, at room temperature, diced

For the filling
6 smoked streaky (fatty) bacon rashers (strips), rinds removed
300ml/½ pint/1¼ cups double (heavy) cream
3 eggs, plus 3 yolks
25g/1oz/2 tbsp unsalted butter
salt and ground black pepper

1 To make the pastry, place the flour, salt, egg yolk and butter in a food processor and process until blended. Turn on to a lightly floured surface and bring the mixture together into a ball. Leave to rest for 20 minutes.

2 Lightly flour a deep 20cm/8in round flan tin (pan), and place it on a baking tray. Roll out the pastry and use to line the tin. Trim off the excess.

> **COOK'S TIP**
> To prepare in advance, bake for 5–10 minutes less than advised, until just set. Reheat at 190°C/375°F/Gas 5 for 10 minutes.

3 Gently press the pastry into the corners of the tin. If the pastry breaks up, just push it into shape. Chill for 20 minutes. Preheat the oven to 200°C/400°F/Gas 6.

4 Meanwhile, cut the bacon rashers into thin pieces and grill until the fat runs. Arrange the bacon in the pastry case (pie shell). Beat together the cream, the whole eggs and yolks and seasoning. Carefully pour into the pastry case.

5 Bake for 15 minutes, then reduce the heat to 180°C/350°F/Gas 4 and bake for a further 15–20 minutes. When the filling is puffed up and golden brown, and the pastry edge crisp, remove from the oven and top with knobs (pats) of butter. Stand for 5 minutes before serving.

Energy 976kcal/4043kJ; Protein 18.1g; Carbohydrate 35.5g, of which sugars 2.2g; Fat 85.8g, of which saturates 48.4g; Cholesterol 519mg; Calcium 149mg; Fibre 1.4g; Sodium 678mg.

Leek and bacon tarts

These versatile tartlets are a favourite of the afternoon tea table. They make a deliciously savoury treat to eat instead of sandwiches. Serve with a mixed leaf salad, which has been tossed in a light lemony dressing. Serve with strong tea.

MAKES 6–8 TARTLETS

275g/10oz/2½ cups plain
  (all-purpose) flour
pinch of salt
175g/6oz/¾ cup butter, diced
2 egg yolks
about 45ml/3 tbsp very cold water
salad leaves, to garnish

For the filling
225g/8oz streaky (fatty) bacon,
  diced
4 leeks, sliced
6 eggs
115g/4oz/½ cup soft white
  (farmer's) cheese
15ml/1 tbsp mild mustard
pinch of cayenne pepper
salt and ground black pepper

1 Sieve (sift) the flour and salt into a bowl, and rub in the butter with your fingertips until it resembles fine breadcrumbs. Alternatively, use a food processor.

2 Add the egg yolks and just enough water to combine the dough. Wrap the dough in clear film (plastic wrap) and place in the refrigerator for 30 minutes.

3 Meanwhile preheat the oven to 200°C/400°F/Gas 6.

4 Roll out the pastry thinly and use to line the tartlet tins (pans). Prick the pastry. Bake for 15–20 minutes.

5 Fry the bacon until crisp. Add the leeks and cook for 3–4 minutes Remove from the heat.

6 In a bowl, beat the eggs, soft cheese, mustard, cayenne pepper and seasoning together, then add the leeks and bacon.

7 Pour the filling into the tartlet tins and bake for 35–40 minutes, until golden. Remove the tartlets from the tins, and serve warm or cold, garnished with salad leaves.

Energy 487kcal/2026kJ; Protein 15.4g; Carbohydrate 28.2g, of which sugars 1.6g; Fat 35.7g, of which saturates 19.1g; Cholesterol 265mg; Calcium 107mg; Fibre 2.1g; Sodium 681mg.

Finger food

Tasty morsels of food tempt the appetite. Serve these sausage rolls, crackers and cheese straws alongside sandwiches, pâtés and cheeses as a filling accompaniment. The salty flavours are a winner with children and adults alike.

Sausage rolls

Small sausage rolls rank high in the league of popular tea-time and party foods. Serve them hot or cold

MAKES ABOUT 16

175g/6oz/1½ cups plain
  (all-purpose) flour
pinch of salt
40g/1½oz/3 tbsp lard, diced
40g/1½oz/3 tbsp butter, diced
250g/9oz pork sausagemeat
  (bulk sausage)
beaten egg, to glaze

1 To make the pastry, sift the flour and salt into a bowl. Rub the fats into the flour until the mixture resembles fine crumbs.

2 Stir in 45ml/3 tbsp cold water and gather into a smooth ball of dough. Wrap with clear film (plastic wrap) and chill for 30 minutes.

COOK'S TIP
Buy pastry readymade if you don't have time to make it.

3 Preheat the oven to 190°C/375°F/ Gas 5. Roll out the pastry on a lightly floured surface to make a rectangle about 30cm/12in long. Cut lengthways into two long strips.

4 Divide the sausagemeat into two pieces and, on a lightly floured surface, shape each into a long roll the same length as the pastry. Place a roll on each strip of pastry. Brush the pastry edges with water and fold them over the meat, pressing the edges together to seal them well.

5 Cut each roll into eight. Turn the rolls over and, with the seam side down and brush with beaten egg. Place on a baking sheet and bake for 30 minutes until crisp and golden. Place on a serving plate and serve hot or transfer to a wire rack to cool.

Energy 125kcal/521kJ; Protein 2.5g; Carbohydrate 10.3g, of which sugars 0.5g; Fat 8.4g, of which saturates 3.9g; Cholesterol 14mg; Calcium 23mg; Fibre 0.4g; Sodium 142mg.

Parmesan thins

These crisp, light, savoury crackers are very moreish – the perfect crunchy bite at tea time.

MAKES 16–20

50g/2oz/½ cup plain (all-purpose) flour
40g/1½oz/3 tbsp butter, softened
1 egg yolk
40g/1½oz/⅔ cup Parmesan cheese, freshly grated
pinch of salt
pinch of mustard powder

1 Rub together the flour and the butter in a bowl, then work in the egg yolk, the cheese, salt and mustard. Mix with a wooden spoon to bring the dough together into a ball. Shape into a log, then wrap in foil or clear film (plastic wrap) and chill for at least 10 minutes.

2 Preheat the oven to 200°C/400°F/Gas 6. Cut the dough log into thin slices, about 3–6mm/ ⅛–¼in, and arrange on a well-greased baking sheet.

3 Flatten with a fork to give a pretty ridged pattern. Bake for 10 minutes or until crisp. Cool on a wire rack.

Energy 36kcal/148kJ; Protein 1.2g; Carbohydrate 2g, of which sugars 0.1g; Fat 2.6g, of which saturates 1.5g; Cholesterol 16mg; Calcium 29mg; Fibre 0.1g; Sodium 34mg.

Cheese straws

These rich cheesy sticks make a fantastic nibble to begin your afternoon tea. Delicious served still warm.

MAKES ABOUT 10

75g/3oz/⅔ cup plain (all-purpose) flour
40g/1½oz/3 tbsp butter, diced
40g/1½ oz mature (sharp) hard cheese, finely grated
1 egg
5ml/1 tsp ready-made mustard
salt and ground black pepper

1 Preheat the oven to 180°C/350°F/Gas 4. Line a baking sheet with baking parchment. Sift the flour, salt and pepper into a bowl. Rub the butter into the flour until the mixture resembles breadcrumbs. Stir in the cheese.

2 Lightly beat the egg with the mustard. Add half the egg to the flour, stirring in until the mixture can be gathered into a smooth ball of dough.

3 Roll out the dough into a 15cm/6in square. Cut into narrow lengths. Place on the baking sheet and brush with the remaining egg. Bake for 12 minutes until golden brown.

Energy 49kcal/206kJ; Protein 1.5g; Carbohydrate 3.9g, of which sugars 0.1g; Fat 3.1g, of which saturates 1.9g; Cholesterol 13mg; Calcium 32mg; Fibre 0.2g; Sodium 39mg.

Teabreads and pastries

This winning collection of sweet and savoury breads, delicate pastries, individual tarts and filled choux buns is a visual feast to behold. Crammed with quality ingredients, these tea-time treats fill the home with sweet aromas as they bake. Who could resist lightly toasted teacakes dripping with melted butter, or soft-centred, nutmeg-infused custard tarts encased in a light and crisp pastry?

Crumpets

Made with a yeast batter and cooked quickly in metal rings on a griddle, crumpets are a particularly traditional English tea-time food with an unusual dense and spongy texture. Serve them freshly toasted and spread with butter and a drizzle of golden syrup or honey.

MAKES ABOUT 10

225g/8oz/2 cups plain (all-purpose) flour
pinch of salt
2.5ml/½ tsp bicarbonate of soda (baking soda)
5ml/1 tsp easy-blend (rapid-rise) dried yeast
150ml/¼ pint/⅔ cup milk
oil, for greasing

1 Sift the flour, salt and bicarbonate of soda into a bowl and stir in the yeast. Make a well in the centre.

2 Heat the milk with 200ml/7fl oz/ scant 1 cup water until lukewarm.

3 Pour the milk into the well and beat or whisk vigorously to make a thick, smooth batter.

4 Cover the bowl with a dish towel and leave in a warm place for about 1 hour until the mixture has a spongy texture.

5 Heat a griddle or heavy frying pan. Lightly oil the hot surface and the inside of three or four metal rings, each measuring about 8cm/3½in in diameter. Place the oiled rings on the hot surface and leave for 1–2 minutes until hot.

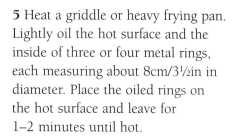

6 Spoon the batter into the rings to a depth of about 1cm/½in. Cook over a medium-high heat for about 6 minutes until the top surface is set and bubbles have burst open to make holes.

7 When set, carefully lift off the metal rings and flip the crumpets over, cooking the second side for just 1 minute until lightly browned.

8 Lift off the griddle and leave to cool completely on a wire rack. Repeat with the remaining crumpet mixture until used up.

9 Just before serving, toast the crumpets on both sides so that the surface is quite hard. Butter the holey surface generously. Crumpets can be served with jam, curd, honey, peanut butter, cheese spread, or just with lashings of butter.

Energy 93kcal/393kJ; Protein 3g; Carbohydrate 16.5g, of which sugars 1g; Fat 2.1g, of which saturates 1g; Cholesterol 21mg; Calcium 48mg; Fibre 0.6g; Sodium 21mg.

English muffins

Unlike their American cousins, which are a type of small cake, English muffins are circles of bread cooked on a griddle, which are made for toasting. They have a bland flavour so are perfect served warm, split open and spread with butter.

MAKES 9

450g/1lb/4 cups unbleached strong
   white bread flour
7.5ml/1½ tsp salt
350–375ml/12–13fl oz/
   1½–1⅔ cups lukewarm milk
pinch of caster (superfine) sugar
15g/½oz fresh yeast
15ml/1 tbsp melted butter or
   olive oil
rice flour or semolina, for dusting

1 Generously flour a non-stick baking sheet and very lightly grease a griddle pan.

2 Sift the flour and salt together into a large bowl and make a well in the centre. Blend 150ml/¼ pint/⅔ cup of the milk, sugar and yeast together. Stir in the remaining milk and butter or oil.

3 Add the yeast mixture to the well and beat for 4–5 minutes until smooth and elastic. The dough will be soft but just hold its shape. Cover with lightly oiled clear film (plastic wrap) and leave to rise in a warm place for 45–60 minutes, or until doubled in bulk.

4 Turn out the dough on to a floured surface and knock back (punch down). Roll out to 1cm/½in thick. Stamp out 7.5cm/3in rounds.

5 Dust the dough rounds with rice flour or semolina and place on the prepared baking sheet. Cover and leave to rise, in a warm place, for about 20–30 minutes.

6 Warm the griddle over a medium heat. Carefully transfer the muffins in batches to the griddle. Cook slowly for about 7 minutes on each side or until golden brown. Transfer to a wire rack to cool. When cold, toast like bread, and serve generously spread with butter.

Energy 201kcal/852kJ; Protein 6g; Carbohydrate 40.7g, of which sugars 2.6g; Fat 2.7g, of which saturates 1.4g; Cholesterol 6mg; Calcium 117mg; Fibre 1.6g; Sodium 356mg.

Drop scones

Variously known as girdle cakes, griddlecakes and Scotch pancakes, these make a quick and easy tea-time snack. Serve them warm with butter and drizzled with honey, maple syrup or golden syrup for a sweet and satisfying, warming treat.

4 Make a well in the centre of the flour mixture, then stir in the egg. Add the milk a little at a time, stirring well after each addition. Add enough milk to give a thick creamy consistency.

5 Cook the batter in batches. Drop 3 or 4 evenly sized spoonfuls of the mixture, spaced slightly apart, on the griddle or frying pan. Cook over a medium heat for 2–3 minutes, until bubbles rise to the surface and burst.

6 Turn the scones over and cook for a further 2–3 minutes, until golden underneath. Place the cooked scones between the folds of a clean dish towel while cooking the remaining batter. Serve warm, with butter and honey or maple syrup.

MAKES 8–10

115g/4oz/1 cup plain
   (all-purpose) flour
5ml/1 tsp bicarbonate of soda
   (baking soda)
5ml/1 tsp cream of tartar
25g/1oz/2 tbsp butter, diced
1 egg, beaten
about 150ml/¼ pint/⅔ cup milk
butter and honey or maple syrup,
   to serve

1 Lightly grease a griddle pan or heavy frying pan, then preheat it over a medium heat.

2 Meanwhile, sift the flour, bicarbonate of soda and cream of tartar together into a mixing bowl.

3 Add the diced butter and rub it into the flour with your fingertips until the mixture resembles fine, evenly sized breadcrumbs.

Energy 59kcal/249kJ; Protein 2g; Carbohydrate 10.9g, of which sugars 1.8g; Fat 1.1g, of which saturates 0.2g; Cholesterol 11mg; Calcium 65mg; Fibre 0.4g; Sodium 56mg.

Tinkers' cakes

These delicate little cakes can be rustled up in no time for eating hot off the stove. The quantities given are small because they must be eaten while really fresh. This is a classic Welsh recipe, but naturally finds a place in the English afternoon tea.

MAKES 8–10

125g/4½oz/1 cup self-raising
(self-rising) flour, plus extra
for dusting
pinch of salt
70g/2½oz/5 tbsp butter, diced, plus
extra for greasing
50g/2oz/4 tbsp demerara (raw) or
light muscovado (brown) sugar
1 small cooking apple, weighing
about 150g/5oz
about 30ml/2 tbsp milk
caster (superfine) sugar, for dusting

1 Preheat a heavy frying pan over low to medium heat.

2 Sift the flour and salt into a mixing bowl. Add the butter and, with your fingertips, rub it into the flour until the mixture resembles fine breadcrumbs. Stir in the sugar.

3 Peel and grate the apple, discarding the core. Stir the grated apple into the flour mixture with enough of the milk to make a mixture that can be gathered into a ball of soft, moist dough. Knead slightly to make sure the ingredients are thoroughly combined.

4 Transfer to a lightly floured surface and roll out the dough to about 5mm/¼in thick. With a 6–7.5cm/ 2½–3in cutter, stamp out rounds, gathering up the offcuts and re-rolling them to make more.

5 Smear a little butter on the hot griddle pan and cook the cakes, in batches, for about 4–5 minutes on each side or until golden brown and cooked through. Lift on to a wire rack and dust with caster sugar. Serve immediately.

VARIATIONS
• Add a good pinch of ground cinnamon or mixed (apple pie) spice to the sifted flour.
• Cut the rolled-out dough into squares or triangles for a change.

Energy 121kcal/508kJ; Protein 1.4g; Carbohydrate 16.5g, of which sugars 6.9g; Fat 6g, of which saturates 3.7g; Cholesterol 15mg; Calcium 26mg; Fibre 0.6g; Sodium 45mg.

Teacakes

These fruit-filled tea-time treats are thought to be a refinement of the original 'handbread': a shaped roll made on a flat tin. You can add 5ml/1 tsp allspice to the flour, if you like. Serve them split and buttered, either warm from the oven or toasted.

MAKES 8–10

450g/1lb/4 cups unbleached (strong) white bread flour
5ml/1 tsp salt
5ml/1 tsp easy-blend (rapid-rise) dried yeast
280ml/10fl oz/1¼ cups milk, luke warm, plus extra, for glazing
40g/1½oz/3 tbsp caster (superfine) sugar
40g/1½oz/3 tbsp butter, diced
50g/2oz/¼ cup currants
50g/2oz/⅓ cup sultanas (golden raisins)

1 Sift the flour and salt into a bowl.

2 In a jug (pitcher) mix the yeast, 5ml/ 1 tsp of the sugar and the lukewarm milk and leave to stand for 5 minutes.

3 Add the remaining sugar to the flour and make a well in the centre. Pour in the milk a little at a time and mix well, adding just enough to make a dry dough. Add the butter and knead briefly.

4 Turn the dough out on to a lightly floured surface and knead vigorously for at least 15 minutes, until the dough is no longer sticky and full of little bubbles, adding a little extra milk if necessary.

5 Shape the dough into a ball, place in a clean bowl and cover with a dampened dish towel. Leave at room temperature for 1 hour, until it has doubled in bulk.

6 Grease two baking sheets.

7 Turn out the dough and knead in the dried fruit until it is evenly distributed. Divide the dough into eight to ten portions, and shape into balls. Flatten each one into a disc about 1cm/½in thick.

8 Place the discs on the baking sheets, 2.5cm/1in apart. Cover with oiled clear film (plastic wrap) and leave in a warm place for 30–45 minutes, or until they have almost doubled in size. Preheat the oven to 200°C/400°F/Gas 6.

9 Brush the top of each teacake with milk, then bake for 15–18 minutes, or until golden. Turn out on to a wire rack to cool slightly. To serve, split open while warm and spread with butter, or let the teacakes cool, then split and toast them.

Energy 239kcal/1011kJ; Protein 5.4g; Carbohydrate 47.4g, of which sugars 13.1g; Fat 4.4g, of which saturates 2.5g; Cholesterol 11mg; Calcium 107mg; Fibre 1.6g; Sodium 245mg.

Barm brack

A cross between cake and bread, this satisfying loaf was traditionally served at Halloween. It has a slightly sweet dough, but without the richness of cake, making it perfect for spreading with butter. Serve it sliced and buttered while still warm from the oven if possible.

MAKES 2 LOAVES

450g/1lb/4 cups plain (all-purpose) flour
5ml/1 tsp mixed (apple pie) spice
pinch of salt
2 sachets easy-blend (rapid-rise) dried yeast
75g/3oz/6 tbsp soft dark brown sugar
115g/4oz/½ cup butter, melted
300ml/½ pint/1¼ cups tepid milk
1 egg, lightly beaten
375g/13oz/generous 2 cups dried mixed fruit
25g/1oz/⅓ cup chopped mixed peel
15ml/1 tbsp caster (superfine) sugar

1 Butter two 450g/1lb loaf tins (pans). Mix the flour, spice, salt, yeast and sugar in a large bowl and make a well in the centre. Mix the butter with the tepid milk and lightly beaten egg and add to the bowl.

2 Add the dried fruit and peel and mix well. Turn the mixture into the loaf tins. Leave in a warm place for about 30 minutes to rise. Preheat the oven to 200°C/400°F/Gas 6.

VARIATION
Soak the dried fruit in weak tea overnight. You could try a flavoured tea for this. The tea is soaked up by the fruit, making it plumper, softer and much more flavoursome.

3 When the dough has doubled in size, bake in the hot oven for about 45 minutes, or until the loaves begin to shrink slightly from the sides of the tins; when turned out and tapped underneath they should sound hollow.

4 To make the glaze, mix the caster sugar with 30ml/2 tbsp boiling water. Brush the glaze liberally over the hot loaves. Return to the oven for 3 minutes, or until the tops are a rich shiny brown. Turn out on to a wire rack to cool.

Energy per loaf 2019kcal/8524kJ; Protein 34.9g; Carbohydrate 364.6g, of which sugars 193.2g; Fat 57g, of which saturates 32.8g; Cholesterol 246mg; Calcium 704mg; Fibre 11.7g; Sodium 590mg.

Apple pie

The rich sweet pastry of this indulgent apple pie has the texture and taste of cake. Serve it with a generous dollop of whipped cream for a slice of apple heaven.

SERVES 6

215g/7½oz/scant 2 cups plain (all-purpose) flour, plus extra for dusting
5ml/1 tsp baking powder
pinch of salt
115g/4oz/½ cup cold unsalted butter, cubed
finely grated rind of ½ lemon
75g/3oz/scant ½ cup caster (superfine) sugar, plus extra for sprinkling
2 small (US medium) eggs
3 eating apples, peeled, cored and diced
ground cinnamon, for sprinkling
whipped cream, to serve

1 Sift the flour, baking powder and salt into a food processor. Add the butter and grated lemon rind and process briefly, then add the sugar, 1 whole egg and 1 yolk to the mixture and process to make a soft dough.

2 Divide the dough into two pieces, one portion nearly double the size of the other. Pat the dough into two flat cakes. Wrap tightly in clear film (plastic wrap) and chill for at least 2 hours until firm.

3 Preheat the oven to 180°C/350°F/Gas 4. Place a baking sheet in the oven and grease a 20cm/8in loose-based flan tin (tart pan).

4 Place the large ball of dough between two lightly floured sheets of clear film. Roll out a 25cm/10in round. Discard the top layer of film and lift the dough on the lower piece. Place it face down in the tin. Peel off the film. Press into the tin so that it stands just clear of the top.

5 Pack with the apples and sprinkle with cinnamon. Roll out the second piece of dough in the same way, to the same size as the tin. Lay the dough on top of the apples and fold the edges of the bottom piece of dough inward, pressing to seal.

6 Prick the dough, brush with egg white and sprinkle with sugar. Place on the hot baking sheet and bake for 20 minutes. Reduce the oven temperature to 160C/325°F/Gas 3 and bake for 25–30 minutes.

Energy 362kcal/1519kJ; Protein 5.8g; Carbohydrate 47g, of which sugars 19.7g; Fat 18.1g, of which saturates 10.6g; Cholesterol 104mg; Calcium 72mg; Fibre 2.2g; Sodium 143mg.

Curd tart

The distinguishing characteristic of curd tart is the distinctive flavour of allspice. The result tastes superb and is not too sweet. Serve with a spoonful of cream, if you like.

SERVES 8

225g/8oz/2 cups plain
 (all-purpose) flour
115g/4oz/½ cup butter, diced
1 egg yolk
15–30ml/1–2 tbsp chilled water

For the filling
90g/3½ oz/scant ½ cup soft light
 brown sugar
large pinch of ground allspice
3 eggs, beaten
grated rind and juice of 1 lemon
40g/1½ oz/3 tbsp butter, melted
450g/1lb/2 cups soft white curd
 (farmer's) cheese
75g/3oz/scant ½ cup raisins

1 To make the pastry, place the flour in a large mixing bowl and rub in the butter until the mixture resembles fine breadcrumbs. Stir the egg yolk into the flour and add just enough of the water to bind the mixture together to form a dough.

2 Place the dough on a lightly floured surface, knead lightly and briefly, then form into a ball. Roll out the pastry to 3mm/⅛in thick and use to line a 20cm/8in fluted loose-based flan tin (quiche pan). Cover with clear film (plastic wrap) and chill for 15 minutes.

COOK'S TIP
Although it is not traditional, mixed (apple pie) spice would make a good substitute for the ground allspice.

3 Preheat the oven to 190°C/ 375°F/Gas 5. Mix the brown sugar with the ground allspice in a bowl, then stir in the beaten eggs, lemon rind and juice, butter, curd cheese and raisins. Mix thoroughly with a wire whisk.

4 Pour the filling into the pastry case (pie shell), then bake for 40 minutes, or until the pastry is cooked and the filling is lightly set and golden brown. Cool slightly, remove from the tin and serve warm or cold.

Energy 480kcal/2005kJ; Protein 16.2g; Carbohydrate 48.2g, of which sugars 23.7g; Fat 27g, of which saturates 15.8g; Cholesterol 173mg; Calcium 153mg; Fibre 1.2g; Sodium 451mg.

Custard tarts

These luxurious little tarts are an indulgent treat. The silky texture of the custard combined with the rich vanilla-flavoured pastry is truly unsurpassable. The nutmeg-dusted delights are perfect served still warm, but can be cooled and kept in the refrigerator for up to two days.

MAKES ABOUT 8

175g/6oz/1½ cups plain
    (all-purpose) flour
pinch of salt
75g/3oz/6 tbsp unsalted butter, at
    room temperature
75g/3oz/6 tbsp caster (superfine)
    sugar
3 egg yolks, at room temperature
a few drops vanilla extract

For the filling
600ml/1 pint/2½ cups full cream
    (whole) milk
6 egg yolks
75g/3oz/6 tbsp caster (superfine)
    sugar
freshly grated nutmeg

1 To make the pastry, sift the flour and salt into a bowl.

2 Put the butter, sugar, egg yolks and vanilla extract in a food processor and process until the mixture resembles scrambled eggs. Add the flour and blend briefly.

3 Transfer the dough to a lightly floured surface and knead gently until smooth. Form into a ball, flatten and wrap in clear film (plastic wrap). Chill for at least 30 minutes. Bring back to room temperature before rolling out.

4 Roll out the pastry and use to line eight individual 10cm/4in loose-bottomed tartlet tins (pans). Place on a baking sheet and chill for 30 minutes.

5 Preheat the oven to 200°C/400°F/ Gas 6. To make the custard filling, gently heat the milk in a pan until just warmed but not yet boiling.

6 In a bowl, vigorously beat the egg yolks and sugar together until they become pale and creamy in texture.

7 Pour the milk on to the yolks and stir well to mix. Do not whisk as this will produce too many bubbles.

8 Strain the milk mixture into a jug (pitcher), then carefully pour the liquid into the tart cases.

9 Liberally grate fresh nutmeg over the surface of the tartlets.

10 Bake for about 10 minutes, then lower the heat to 180°C/350°F/ Gas 4 and bake for another 10 minutes, or until the filling has set and is just turning golden. The tartlets should be a bit wobbly when they come out of the oven.

11 Remove from the oven and lift the tarts out of the tins. Serve warm or cold.

Energy 336kcal/1409kJ; Protein 7.9g; Carbohydrate 40g, of which sugars 23.4g; Fat 17.1g, of which saturates 8.6g; Cholesterol 257mg; Calcium 157mg; Fibre 0.7g; Sodium 101mg.

Jam tarts

These nostalgic jam tarts are the perfect treat for children. Fill them with your favourite varieties of jam, homemade if possible, such as strawberry, raspberry and apricot.

2 Preheat the oven to 220°C/425°F/ Gas 7. Lightly grease a 12-hole (or two 6-hole) tartlet tins (muffin pans).

3 Roll out the pastry on a lightly floured surface to about 3mm/⅛in thick and, using a 7.5cm/3in cutter, stamp out 12 circles. Gather the trimmings and roll and cut out more.

4 Press the pastry circles into the prepared tartlet tin. Place a heaped teaspoonful of jam into the centre of each one.

MAKES 12

175g/6oz/1½ cups plain (all-
    purpose) flour
pinch of salt
30ml/2 tbsp caster (superfine)
    sugar
85g/3oz/6 tbsp butter, diced
1 egg, lightly beaten
60–75ml/4–5 tbsp jam

VARIATION
Replace the jam with orange, lemon or lime curd, or you could try chocolate spread.

1 Sift the flour, salt and sugar into a bowl. Rub in the butter until the mixture resembles fine crumbs. Stir in the egg and gather into a smooth dough ball. Wrap in clear film (plastic wrap) and chill for 30 minutes.

5 Put the tartlet tin into the hot oven and bake for 15–20 minutes until the pastry is cooked through and light golden brown in colour. Carefully lift the tarts out of the tin on to a wire rack and leave to cool before serving.

Energy 114kcal/479kJ; Protein 1.1g; Carbohydrate 18.8g, of which sugars 12.5g; Fat 4.3g, of which saturates 2.6g; Cholesterol 18mg; Calcium 16mg; Fibre 0.3g; Sodium 39mg.

Bakewell tart

Although the pastry base is made of puff pastry, you could substitute a sweet, rich shortcrust pastry instead. The frangipane topping of ground almonds, sugar and butter is not too sweet.

SERVES 4

225g/8oz puff pastry dough
30ml/2 tbsp raspberry or apricot
  jam
2 eggs, plus 2 egg yolks
115g/4oz/½ cup caster (superfine)
  sugar
115g/4oz/½ cup butter, melted
50g/2oz/⅔ cup ground almonds
a few drops almond extract
icing (confectioners') sugar,
  for dusting

1 Preheat the oven to 200°C/400°F/
Gas 6.

2 Roll out the pastry on a lightly floured surface and use to line an 18cm/7in tart tin (pan). Trim the edges with a sharp knife.

3 Prick the pastry case (pie shell) all over, then spread jam over the base.

COOK'S TIP
Place a baking sheet in the oven to heat up while the oven preheats. Place the tart on the tray. This will ensure that the pastry base cooks right through.

4 Whisk the eggs, egg yolks and sugar together in a bowl until thick and pale. Stir the melted butter, ground almonds and almond extract into the whisked egg mixture.

5 Pour the mixture into the pastry case and bake for 30 minutes, or until the filling is just set and lightly browned. Dust with icing sugar before serving hot, warm or cold.

Energy 700kcal/2919kJ; Protein 10.8g; Carbohydrate 57.1g, of which sugars 36.7g; Fat 49.9g, of which saturates 17.1g; Cholesterol 257mg; Calcium 110mg; Fibre 0.9g; Sodium 394mg.

Treacle tart

Traditional shortcrust pastry is perfect for this old-fashioned tart, with its sticky lemon and golden syrup filling and twisted lattice topping. It's delicious served warm or cold with cream or custard.

3 Put a baking sheet in the oven and preheat to 200°C/400°F/Gas 6. To make the filling, warm the syrup in a pan until it melts.

4 Remove the syrup from the heat and stir in the breadcrumbs and lemon rind. Leave to stand for 10 minutes, then add more breadcrumbs if it is too runny. Stir in the lemon juice, then spread evenly in the pastry case.

SERVES 4–6

150g/5oz/1¼ cups plain (all-purpose) flour
pinch of salt
130g/4½oz/9 tbsp chilled butter, diced
45–60ml/3–4 tbsp chilled water

For the filling
260g/9½oz/generous ¾ cup golden (light corn) syrup
about 75g/3oz/1½ cups fresh white breadcrumbs
grated rind of 1 lemon
30ml/2 tbsp lemon juice
cream or custard, to serve

1 To make the pastry, combine the flour and salt in a bowl. Rub in the butter until the mixture resembles coarse crumbs. With a fork, stir in enough water to bind the dough. Gather into a ball, knead lightly for a few seconds until smooth then wrap in clear film (plastic wrap) and chill for 20 minutes.

2 On a lightly floured surface, roll out the pastry to a thickness of 3mm/⅛in. Use to line a 20cm/8in fluted flan tin (quiche pan) and trim off the overhang. Chill the pastry case (pie shell) for 20 minutes. Reserve the pastry trimmings.

5 Roll out the pastry trimmings and cut into 10–12 thin strips. Twist the strips and arrange half on the filling and the rest at right angles to form a lattice. Press the ends on to the rim.

6 Place the tart on the hot baking sheet and bake for 10 minutes. Lower the oven temperature to 190°C/375°F/Gas 5. Bake for 15 minutes more, until golden.

Energy 420kcal/1764kJ; Protein 4.1g; Carbohydrate 63.5g, of which sugars 35.1g; Fat 18.4g, of which saturates 11.3g; Cholesterol 46mg; Calcium 62mg; Fibre 1.1g; Sodium 344mg.

Border tart

This rich and sweet fruity tart comes from the border region of England and Scotland. It is good served hot or cold with a spoonful of cream on the side.

SERVES 4

150g/5oz/10 tbsp butter
50g/2oz/¼ cup caster (superfine) sugar
225g/8oz/2 cups plain (all-purpose) flour
1 egg, beaten

For the filling
1 egg, beaten
75g/3oz/scant ½ cup soft light brown sugar
50g/2oz/¼ cup butter, melted
10ml/2 tsp white wine vinegar
115g/4oz/½ cup currants
25g/1oz/¼ cup chopped walnuts
double (heavy) cream, to serve

1 Make the pastry: cream the butter with the sugar in a large bowl. Add the flour and egg. Mix until just combined. Wrap in clear film (plastic wrap) and chill for 1 hour.

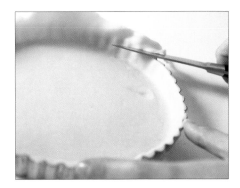

2 Roll out the pastry and use to line a 20cm/8in flan tin (tart pan). Trim the edges neatly.

3 Preheat the oven to 190°C/375°F/ Gas 5. To make the filling, in a large bowl, mix together the egg, sugar and butter.

4 Stir the vinegar, currants and walnuts into the egg mixture.

VARIATION
The white wine vinegar can be replaced with lemon juice if you prefer a citrus flavour.

5 Pour the mixture into the pastry case (pie shell) and bake in the preheated oven for 30 minutes.

6 Leave to stand for a few minutes, then remove from the tin and leave to cool on a wire rack for at least 30 minutes. Serve with a dollop of fresh cream.

Energy 312kcal/1307kJ; Protein 3.4g; Carbohydrate 41.1g, of which sugars 41g; Fat 16.1g, of which saturates 7.3g; Cholesterol 74mg; Calcium 54mg; Fibre 0.8g; Sodium 99mg.

Summer berry tart

A simple crisp pastry case is all that is needed to set off this classic filling of vanilla-flavoured custard, topped with luscious berry fruits and drizzled with syrup. Use whatever fruits are available locally for a colourful tart bursting with summer freshness.

SERVES 6–8

185g/6¼oz/1⅔ cups plain (all-purpose) flour
pinch of salt
115g/4oz/½ cup butter, diced
1 egg yolk
30ml/2 tbsp chilled water

For the filling
3 egg yolks
50g/2oz/¼ cup caster (superfine) sugar
30ml/2 tbsp cornflour (cornstarch)
30ml/2 tbsp plain (all-purpose) flour
5ml/1 tsp vanilla extract
300ml/½ pint/1¼ cups milk
150ml/¼ pint/⅔ cup double (heavy) cream
800g/1¾lb/7 cups mixed summer berries
60ml/4 tbsp redcurrant jelly
30ml/2 tbsp raspberry liqueur

1 To make the pastry, sift the flour and salt into a mixing bowl. Rub in the butter until the mixture resembles fine breadcrumbs. Mix the egg yolk with the chilled water and sprinkle over the dry ingredients. Mix to a firm dough.

2 Knead the dough on a lightly floured surface for a few seconds, until smooth. Wrap in clear film (plastic wrap) and chill for 30 minutes.

3 Roll out the pastry and use to line a 23cm/9in round flan tin (tart pan). Wrap in clear film and chill.

4 Preheat the oven to 200°C/400°F/Gas 6. Prick the base of the pastry, line it with baking parchment, fill with baking beans and bake on a tray for 15 minutes. Remove the baking parchment and beans and bake for 10 minutes more. Leave to cool.

COOK'S TIP
Dust the tart with icing (confectioners') sugar, if you like.

5 To make the filling, beat the egg yolks, sugar, cornflour, flour and vanilla together in a large bowl.

6 Pour the milk into a pan, and heat gently until almost boiling. Slowly pour the milk on to the egg mixture, whisking all the time.

7 Pour the custard back from the bowl into the pan and stir constantly over a low heat, until it has thickened. Work quickly or lumps will form. Return to a clean mixing bowl, cover the surface with a piece of clear film and set aside to cool.

8 Whip the cream until thick, then fold into the cooled custard. Spoon the custard into the pastry case (pie shell) and spread out evenly.

9 Wash and dry the fruit, then arrange it on top of the custard.

10 In a small pan, gently heat the redcurrant jelly and liqueur together until melted. Allow to cool, then brush liberally over the surface of the fruit. Serve the tart within 3 hours of assembling. Serve with cream for a decadent treat.

Energy 432kcal/1807kJ; Protein 6.7g; Carbohydrate 47.6g, of which sugars 21.8g; Fat 25.7g, of which saturates 14.6g; Cholesterol 160mg; Calcium 130mg; Fibre 2g; Sodium 150mg.

Chocolate éclairs

These crisp choux pastry fingers are filled with fresh cream, which is slightly sweetened and flavoured with vanilla. The finishing touch to the éclairs is a thick, glossy coat of dark chocolate.

MAKES 12

65g/2½oz/9 tbsp plain
   (all-purpose) flour
pinch of salt
50g/2oz/¼ cup butter, diced
150ml/¼ pint/⅔ cup water
2 eggs, lightly beaten

For the filling and topping
300ml/½ pint/1¼ cups double
   (heavy) cream
10ml/2 tsp icing (confectioners')
   sugar, sifted
1.5ml/¼ tsp vanilla extract
115g/4oz plain (semisweet)
   chocolate
30ml/2 tbsp water
25g/1oz/2 tbsp butter

1 Preheat the oven to 200°C/400°F/ Gas 6. Grease a large baking sheet and line it with baking parchment.

2 To make the pastry, sift the flour and salt on to a small sheet of baking parchment.

3 Heat the butter and water in a pan very gently until the butter melts. Increase the heat and bring to a rolling boil. Remove the pan from the heat and add all the flour. Beat vigorously with a wooden spoon until the flour is incorporated.

COOK'S TIP
When melting the chocolate, ensure that the bowl does not touch the hot water and keep the heat low.

4 Return the pan to a low heat, then beat the mixture until it leaves the sides of the pan and forms a ball. Set the pan aside and allow to cool for 2–3 minutes.

5 Add the beaten eggs a little at a time, beating well after each addition, until you have a smooth, shiny paste, which is thick enough to hold its shape.

6 Spoon the choux pastry into a piping (pastry) bag fitted with a 2.5cm/1in plain nozzle. Pipe 10cm/4in lengths on to the prepared baking sheet. Use a wet knife to cut off the pastry at the nozzle.

7 Bake for 25–30 minutes, or until the pastry fingers are well risen and golden brown in colour. Remove from the oven.

8 Make a neat slit along the side of each to release the steam. Lower the oven temperature to 180°C/350°F/ Gas 4 and bake for a further 5 minutes. Cool on a wire rack.

9 To make the filling, whip the cream with the icing sugar and vanilla extract until it just holds its shape. Spoon into a piping bag fitted with a 1cm/½in plain nozzle and use to fill the éclairs.

10 Place the chocolate and water in a small bowl set over a pan of simmering water until melted. Remove from the heat and gradually stir in the butter. Dip the top of each éclair in the melted chocolate, then place on a rack. Leave in a cool place until the chocolate is set. Best served within 2 hours of making, but can be chilled for 24 hours if required.

Energy 253kcal/1046kJ; Protein 2.7g; Carbohydrate 10.8g, of which sugars 6.5g; Fat 22.4g, of which saturates 13.5g; Cholesterol 86mg; Calcium 30mg; Fibre 0.4g; Sodium 58mg.

Biscuits, bars and small cakes

A small treat for any time of day, biscuits and bars are packed with flavour and sweetness. Eaten with tea following a savoury sandwich, they will stave off hunger pangs in the late afternoon. Try rich, chocolatey fingers, fragrant tea biscuits, or classic lemon shortbread. If you like soft-centred treats, fruity fat rascals or coconut macaroons are just the thing, or for the ultimate finale to afternoon tea, choose freshly baked scones loaded with homemade jam and a dollop of thick cream.

Tea fingers

The unusual ingredient in these cookies is Lady Grey tea – similar to Earl Grey but with the addition of Seville orange and lemon peel, which imparts a subtle citrus flavour.

3 Using your hands, roll the dough on a lightly floured surface into a log, about 23cm/9in long.

4 Gently press down on the top of the log with the palm of your hand to flatten slightly. Wrap the dough in clear film (plastic wrap) and chill for about 1 hour until the dough is firm enough to slice.

5 Using a sharp knife, cut the dough log widthways into 5mm/¼in slices and place, slightly apart, on the prepared baking sheets.

6 Sprinkle the cookies with a little demerara sugar, then bake for 10–15 minutes until lightly browned. Using a palette knife (metal spatula), transfer the cookies to a wire rack and leave to cool.

MAKES ABOUT 36

150g/5oz/10 tbsp unsalted butter, diced and softened
115g/4oz/generous ½ cup light muscovado (brown) sugar
15–30ml/1–2 tbsp Lady Grey tea leaves
1 egg, beaten
200g/7oz/1¾ cups plain (all-purpose) flour
demerara (raw) sugar, for sprinkling

1 Preheat the oven to 190°C/375°F/Gas 5. Line two or three baking sheets with baking parchment.

2 In a large bowl, beat the butter with the sugar until light and creamy. Stir in the tea leaves until well combined. Add the beaten egg, then carefully fold in the flour using a metal spoon.

VARIATION
You could use other exotic types of tea for making these cookies. Try Earl Grey, flavoured with bergamot, Rose Congou, or aromatic flower or fruit teas, such as jasmine, passion fruit, chrysanthemum or strawberry.

Energy 65kcal/270kJ; Protein 0.7g; Carbohydrate 7.7g, of which sugars 3.4g; Fat 3.7g, of which saturates 2.2g; Cholesterol 14mg; Calcium 11mg; Fibre 0.2g; Sodium 28mg.

Shortbread

This easy recipe makes a very light, crisp shortbread with an excellent flavour that keeps well. The lemon rind and almonds are delicious additions, but not usually used in traditional shortbread.

MAKES ABOUT 48

275g/10oz/2½ cups plain
  (all-purpose) flour
25g/1oz/¼ cup ground almonds
225g/8oz/1 cup butter, softened
75g/3oz/6 tbsp caster (superfine)
  sugar
grated rind of ½ lemon

1 Preheat the oven to 180°C/350°F/Gas 4 and grease a large Swiss roll tin (jelly roll pan).

2 Sift the flour and almonds into a bowl. In another bowl, beat the butter, sugar and lemon rind together until the mixture is soft and light. Add the flour and almonds to the butter mixture, then work it together first using a wooden spoon and then your fingers to make a smooth dough.

VARIATIONS
• Replace the lemon rind with the grated rind of two oranges.
• Use a flat decorative mould and make one large shortcake for an attractive, professional-looking result.

3 Place the dough in the tin and flatten out. Bake for 20 minutes, or until pale golden brown.

COOK'S TIP
Use a food processor for speed.

4 Remove from the oven and immediately cut the shortbread into fingers or squares while the mixture is soft. Allow to cool a little, and then transfer to a wire rack and leave until cold. If stored in an airtight container, the shortbread should keep for up to two weeks.

Energy 57kcal/239kJ; Protein 0.8g; Carbohydrate 5.6g, of which sugars 1.2g; Fat 3.7g, of which saturates 2g; Cholesterol 8mg; Calcium 12mg; Fibre 0.3g; Sodium 22mg.

Melting moments

As the name suggests, these crisp biscuits really do melt in the mouth. They have a texture like shortbread but are covered in rolled oats to give a crunchy surface and extra flavour, and are traditionally topped with a piece of cherry.

2 Sift the flour over the mixture and stir to make a soft dough. Gather up the dough, divide into 16–20 pieces and roll into small balls.

3 Spread rolled oats on a sheet of baking parchment and toss the balls in them until evenly coated.

4 Space the dough balls slightly apart, on two baking sheets. Flatten each ball a little with your thumb.

5 Cut the cherries into quarters and place a piece on top of each flat ball. Bake for 15–20 minutes, until they are lightly browned.

6 Allow the biscuits to cool for a few minutes on the baking sheets before transferring them to a wire rack to cool completely.

MAKES 16–20

40g/1½oz/3 tbsp butter, at room temperature
65g/2½oz/5 tbsp lard
85g/3oz/6 tbsp caster (superfine) sugar
1 egg yolk, beaten
few drops of vanilla or almond extract
150g/5oz/1¼ cups self-raising (self-rising) flour
rolled oats, for coating
4–5 glacé (candied) cherries

1 Preheat the oven to 180°C/350°F/ Gas 4. Beat together the butter, lard and sugar, then beat in the egg yolk and vanilla or almond extract.

Energy 88kcal/370kJ; Protein 0.7g; Carbohydrate 10.9g, of which sugars 5.4g; Fat 5g, of which saturates 2.4g; Cholesterol 7mg; Calcium 30mg; Fibre 0.3g; Sodium 40mg.

Oat biscuits

These crisp and crunchy biscuits are wonderfully quick and easy to make, as well as being utterly delicious. They are homely and comforting at any time of day, and are filling enough to keep hunger pangs at bay. Perfect with a cup of tea.

MAKES ABOUT 18

115g/4oz/½ cup butter
115g/4oz/½ cup soft light brown sugar
115g/4oz/½ cup golden (light corn) syrup
150g/5oz/1¼ cups self-raising (self-rising) flour
150g/5oz rolled oats

1 Preheat the oven to 180°C/ 350°F/Gas 4. Lightly grease or line two or three baking sheets with baking parchment.

2 Gently heat the butter, sugar and golden syrup in a heavy pan until the butter has melted and the sugar has dissolved, taking care not to let it get too hot as the mixture will easily burn. Remove from the heat and leave to cool slightly.

VARIATION
Add 25g/1oz/¼ cup finely chopped toasted almonds or walnuts, or a small handful of dried fruit (raisins or sultanas) to the mixture in step 3.

3 Sift the flour and stir into the mixture in the pan, together with the oats, to make a soft dough.

4 Roll the dough into small balls and arrange them on the prepared baking sheets, leaving plenty of room for them to spread out.

5 Flatten each ball with a spatula. Bake for 12–15 minutes until golden brown, longer if more than one tray is in the oven.

6 Leave to cool on the baking sheet briefly, then transfer to a wire rack to crisp up and cool completely.

Energy 151kcal/637kJ; Protein 1.8g; Carbohydrate 23.9g, of which sugars 11.9g; Fat 6g, of which saturates 3.3g; Cholesterol 14mg; Calcium 22mg; Fibre 0.8g; Sodium 59mg.

Jam sandwich biscuits

These buttery cookies are an absolute classic. Sandwiched with buttercream and a generous dollop of strawberry jam, they make a perfect treat for afternoon tea.

MAKES 20

225g/8oz/2 cups plain (all-purpose) flour
175g/6oz/¾ cup unsalted butter, chilled and diced
130g/4½oz/⅔ cup caster (superfine) sugar
1 egg yolk

For the filling
50g/2oz/¼ cup unsalted butter, at room temperature, diced
130g/4½oz/scant 1 cup icing (confectioners') sugar
60–75ml/4–5 tbsp strawberry jam

1 Put the flour and butter in a food processor and process until the mixture resembles breadcrumbs.

2 Add the sugar and egg yolk and process until the mixture starts to form a dough.

3 Turn out on to a floured surface and knead until smooth. Shape into a ball, wrap in clear film (plastic wrap) and chill for at least 30 minutes.

4 Preheat the oven to 180°C/350°F/Gas 4. Lightly grease two baking sheets.

5 Roll out the dough thinly on a lightly floured surface and stamp out rounds using a 6cm/2½in cookie cutter. Re-roll the trimmings and cut out more rounds until you have 40 or an even number.

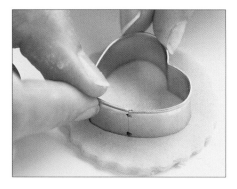

6 Place half the cookie rounds on a prepared baking sheet. Using a small heart-shaped cutter, about 2cm/¾in in diameter, cut out the centres of the remaining rounds. Place these rounds on the second baking sheet.

7 Bake the cookies for 12 minutes until pale golden, then transfer to a wire rack and leave to go completely cold.

8 To make the buttercream filling, beat together the butter and icing sugar until smooth and creamy.

9 Using a palette knife (metal spatula), spread a little buttercream on to each whole cookie. Spoon a little jam on to the buttercream, then gently press the cut-out cookies on top, so that the jam fills the heart-shaped hole.

Energy 166kcal/695kJ; Protein 1.2g; Carbohydrate 22.4g, of which sugars 13.8g; Fat 8.6g, of which saturates 5.4g; Cholesterol 22mg; Calcium 24mg; Fibre 0.4g; Sodium 65mg.

Ginger biscuits

These warming ginger biscuits have a wonderful crispness to them, giving a satisfying 'snap' when broken in half. You can use any shape of cookie cutter you wish.

MAKES ABOUT 50

150g/5oz/10 tbsp plus
  45ml/3 tbsp butter
400g/14oz/2 cups sugar
50ml/2fl oz/¼ cup golden
  (light corn) syrup
15ml/1 tbsp black treacle
  (molasses)
15ml/1 tbsp ground ginger
30ml/2 tbsp ground cinnamon
15ml/1 tbsp ground cloves
5ml/1 tsp ground cardamom
5ml/1 tsp bicarbonate of soda
  (baking soda)
240ml/8fl oz/1 cup water
150g/5oz/1¼ cups plain
  (all-purpose) flour

1 Put the butter, sugar, syrup, treacle, ginger, cinnamon, cloves and cardamom in a heavy pan and heat gently until the butter has melted. Stir thoroughly to combine.

2 Put the bicarbonate of soda and water in a large heatproof bowl. Pour in the warm spice mixture and mix well together, then add the flour and stir until well blended.

3 Cover with clear film (plastic wrap) and chill overnight.

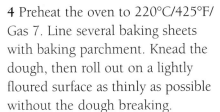

4 Preheat the oven to 220°C/425°F/ Gas 7. Line several baking sheets with baking parchment. Knead the dough, then roll out on a lightly floured surface as thinly as possible without the dough breaking.

5 Stamp out shapes of your choice and place on the baking sheets. Bake for about 5 minutes until golden brown, cooking in batches until all the dough is used. Transfer to wire racks to go completely cold.

Energy 57kcal/239kJ; Protein 0.6g; Carbohydrate 10.3g, of which sugars 6.8g; Fat 1.7g, of which saturates 1g; Cholesterol 7mg; Calcium 16mg; Fibre 0.1g; Sodium 15mg.

Almond cookies

Crystallized petals of alpine pinks, rose petals, primroses or violets make these delicious almond cookies a fragrant and attractive treat to grace the most elegant of tea tables.

3 Add the ground almonds, egg yolk, vanilla and flour. Knead the mixture until blended.

4 Roll the dough into 2.5cm/1in balls, then place on a baking sheet. Brush with lightly beaten egg white and bake for 15 minutes, until golden. Cool on a wire rack.

MAKES ABOUT 24

115g/4oz/½ cup butter
115g/4oz/ generous ½ cup caster (superfine) sugar
115g/4oz/1 cup ground almonds
1 egg, separated
5ml/1 tsp vanilla extract
115g/4oz /1 cup plain (all-purpose) flour, sifted
50g/2oz/½ cup icing (confectioners') sugar

For the crystallized petals
75–100 alpine pink or violet petals
1 egg white, lightly beaten
50g/2oz/½ cup caster (superfine) sugar

1 Preheat the oven to 180°C/ 350°F/Gas 4. Lightly grease two baking sheets.

2 In a large bowl, beat together the butter and caster sugar until light and fluffy. Use a food processor or electric beater for speed, if you like.

CAUTION
Raw eggs should not be consumed by pregnant women, the young and elderly.

5 For the crystallized petals, remove the white heels at the base of each petal. Paint the front and back of each with the egg white. Dredge both sides with caster sugar. Arrange on baking parchment and leave to dry in a warm place. These will last for up to 2 days.

6 To decorate the cookies, mix the icing sugar with 7.5ml/1½ tsp water and spoon on to each cookie, then fix 2–3 petals on top of each one.

Energy 115kcal/481kJ; Protein 1.5g; Carbohydrate 15g, of which sugars 10.1g; Fat 5.8g, of which saturates 2.4g; Cholesterol 9mg; Calcium 24mg; Fibre 0.5g; Sodium 27mg.

Dark chocolate fingers

With their understated elegance and distinctly grown-up flavour, these moreishly decadent chocolate fingers are perfect for a stylish afternoon tea.

MAKES ABOUT 26

115g/4oz/1 cup plain (all-purpose) flour
pinch of baking powder
30ml/2 tbsp unsweetened cocoa powder
50g/2oz/¼ cup caster (superfine) sugar
50g/2oz/¼ cup unsalted butter, softened
20ml/4 tsp golden (light corn) syrup
150g/5oz dark (bittersweet) chocolate
chocolate mini flakes, for sprinkling

1 Preheat the oven to 160°C/325°F/ Gas 3. Line two baking sheets with baking parchment.

2 Sift the dry ingredients into a bowl. Add the butter and golden syrup and work the ingredients together with your hands to form a dough.

VARIATION
Use plain (semisweet) or milk chocolate, if you like.

3 Roll the dough out between sheets of baking parchment to an 18 x 24cm/7 x 9in rectangle. Remove the top sheet. Cut in half lengthways, then into bars 2cm/4in wide. Place on the baking sheets.

4 Bake for about 15 minutes. Transfer to a wire rack to cool.

COOK'S TIP
Do not allow the bars to brown or they will taste bitter.

5 Melt the chocolate in a heatproof bowl set over a pan of simmering water. Half-dip the cookies, place on baking parchment, sprinkle with chocolate flakes, then leave to set.

Energy 72kcal/303kJ; Protein 0.9g; Carbohydrate 9.9g, of which sugars 6.3g; Fat 3.5g, of which saturates 2.1g; Cholesterol 4mg; Calcium 11mg; Fibre 0.4g; Sodium 25mg.

Fat rascals

These delicious cakes are a cross between a scone and a rock cake and are really simple to make. Serve them warm or cold, just as they are or spread with butter.

MAKES 10

350g/12oz/3 cups self-raising (self-rising) flour
175g/6oz/¾ cup butter, diced
115g/4oz/½ cup caster (superfine) sugar
75g/3oz/⅓ cup mixed currants, raisins and sultanas (golden raisins)
25g/1oz/1½ tbsp chopped mixed peel
50g/2oz/⅓ cup glacé (candied) cherries
50g/2oz/⅓ cup blanched almonds, roughly chopped
1 egg
about 75ml/5 tbsp milk

1 Preheat the oven to 200°C/400°F/ Gas 6. Line a baking sheet with baking parchment.

2 Sift the flour into a large bowl. Rub the butter into the flour until the mixture resembles fine breadcrumbs (alternatively whiz the ingredients in a food processor).

3 Stir in the sugar, dried fruit, peel, cherries and almonds.

4 In a small bowl, lightly beat the egg and stir into the flour mixture a spoonful at a time. Add sufficient milk to gather the mixture into a ball of dough, mopping up all the dry ingredients. The dough should have a soft texture, but not be too wet.

5 With lightly floured hands, divide the dough into ten balls, press them into rough circles about 2cm/¾in thick and arrange with plenty of space between them on the prepared baking sheet.

6 Cook for 15–20 minutes until risen and golden brown. Transfer to a wire rack to cool. Store in an airtight container for 2–3 days.

Energy 375kcal/1574kJ; Protein 5.6g; Carbohydrate 50g, of which sugars 23.2g; Fat 18.4g, of which saturates 9.6g; Cholesterol 57mg; Calcium 93mg; Fibre 1.8g; Sodium 129mg.

Soul cakes

These simple cakes originated in the county of Shropshire, England, and were served on All Souls' Day (2 November). They make an unpretentious addition to the tea table.

MAKES ABOUT 20

450g/1lb/4 cups self-raising (self-rising) flour
5ml/1 tsp ground mixed (apple pie) spice
pinch of ground ginger
175g/6oz/¾ cup butter, softened
175g/6oz/¾ cup caster (superfine) sugar, plus extra for sprinkling
2 eggs, lightly beaten
50g/2oz/¼ cup currants, raisins or sultanas (golden raisins)
about 30ml/2 tbsp warm milk

1 Preheat the oven to 180°C/350°F/ Gas 4. Lightly grease two baking sheets or line with baking parchment. Sift the flour and spices into a bowl, and set aside. In a large bowl, beat the butter and sugar until the mixture is light, pale and fluffy.

2 Gradually beat the eggs into the butter mixture. Fold in the flour and the dried fruit, then add sufficient warm milk to bind the mixture and gather it up into a ball of soft dough.

3 Transfer to a lightly floured surface and roll out to about 5mm/¼in thick. Cut into 7.5cm/3in rounds, rolling the trimmings into more.

4 Arrange the cakes on the prepared baking sheets. Prick the surface of the cakes lightly with a fork then, with the back of a knife, mark a deep cross on top of each.

5 Put the cakes into the hot oven and cook for about 15 minutes until risen and golden brown.

6 Sprinkle the cooked cakes with a little caster sugar and then transfer to a wire rack to cool.

COOK'S TIP
The original recipe for these would have contained plain (all-purpose) flour, but self-raising produces a lighter result.

Energy 191kcal/803kJ; Protein 2.9g; Carbohydrate 28.4g, of which sugars 11.3g; Fat 8.1g, of which saturates 4.8g; Cholesterol 38mg; Calcium 45mg; Fibre 0.7g; Sodium 62mg.

Scones with jam and cream

The contrast of warm, buttered scone, homemade jam bursting with fruit, and thick clotted cream is the quintessential taste of English afternoon tea.

MAKES 12

450g/1lb/4 cups self-raising (self-rising) flour or 450g/1lb/4 cups plain (all-purpose) flour and 10ml/2 tsp baking powder
pinch of salt
50g/2oz/¼ cup butter, chilled and diced
15ml/1 tbsp lemon juice
about 400ml/14fl oz/1⅔ cups milk, plus extra to glaze
fruit jam and clotted cream, or whipped cream, to serve

1 Preheat the oven to 230°C/450°F/Gas 8.

2 Sift the flour, salt and baking powder, if using, into a mixing bowl. Rub in the butter with your fingertips until the mixture resembles fine breadcrumbs.

3 In a small bowl, whisk the lemon juice into the milk and leave for about 1 minute to thicken slightly, then pour into the flour mixture and mix quickly to form a soft dough.

4 Knead the dough lightly to form a ball, then roll it out on a floured surface to a thickness of about 2.5cm/1in.

5 Using a 5cm/2in cutter and dipping it into flour each time, stamp out 12 scones, and place them on a well-floured baking sheet. Re-roll any trimmings and cut out more if you can.

6 Brush the tops of the scones lightly with a little milk and then bake them for about 20 minutes, or until risen and golden brown.

7 Wrap the scones in a clean dish towel to keep them warm and soft until ready to serve. Eat with your favourite fruit jam and a generous dollop of clotted cream, or whipped cream if you prefer.

Energy 177kcal/749kJ; Protein 4.7g; Carbohydrate 30.7g, of which sugars 2.2g; Fat 4.8g, of which saturates 2.8g; Cholesterol 12mg; Calcium 93mg; Fibre 1.2g; Sodium 43mg.

Buttermilk scones

These deliciously light, not-too-sweet, scones are a favourite for afternoon tea, served fresh from the oven with butter and homemade jam.

MAKES 18 SMALL SCONES

450g/1lb/4 cups plain (all-purpose) flour
pinch of salt
5ml/1 tsp bicarbonate of soda (baking soda)
50g/2oz/1/4 cup butter, at room temperature, diced
15ml/1 tbsp caster (superfine) sugar
1 small (US medium) egg, lightly beaten
about 300ml/1/2 pint/1 1/4 cups buttermilk

1 Preheat the oven to 220°C/425°F/ Gas 7. Grease two baking sheets.

2 Sift the flour, salt and bicarbonate of soda into a mixing bowl. Rub in the butter until the mixture resembles fine breadcrumbs. Add the sugar and mix well. Make a well in the middle and add the egg and enough buttermilk to mix lightly into a soft dough.

VARIATION
Use half white and half wholemeal (whole-wheat) flour.

3 Turn on to a floured surface and knead lightly into shape. Roll out to about 1cm/1/2in thick.

4 Stamp out 18 scones with a fluted cutter, gathering the trimmings and lightly re-rolling as necessary. Arrange the scones on the baking sheets, spacing well apart.

5 Bake in the preheated oven for about 15–20 minutes, until the scones are well risen and golden brown, reversing the position of the sheets halfway through cooking. Cool on wire racks. Serve warm with butter and jam.

Energy 120kcal/503kJ; Protein 2.7g; Carbohydrate 18.3g, of which sugars 1.1g; Fat 4.5g, of which saturates 2.7g; Cholesterol 11mg; Calcium 54mg; Fibre 0.7g; Sodium 235mg.

Coconut macaroons

Finely grated creamed coconut is combined with the desiccated variety to give these soft-centred cakes a rich creaminess. Made with minimal ingredients, these melt-in-the-mouth macaroons can be made in no time for an uplifting treat on a rainy afternoon.

MAKES 16–18

50g/2oz/1 cup creamed coconut (US thick coconut milk), chilled
2 large (US extra large) egg whites
90g/3¼oz/¼ cup caster (superfine) sugar
75g/3oz/1 cup desiccated (dry unsweetened shredded) coconut

VARIATIONS
• For a tangy flavour, add the grated rind of a lime in step 2.
• Baking the gooey mixture on baking parchment makes sure that the cookies are easily removed from the baking sheet.

1 Preheat the oven to 180°C/350°F/ Gas 4. Line a large baking sheet with baking parchment. Finely grate the creamed coconut.

2 Using an electric beater, whisk the egg whites in a large bowl until stiff. Then whisk in the sugar, a little at a time, to make a stiff and glossy meringue. Fold in the grated, creamed and the desiccated coconut, using a large, metal spoon.

3 Place dessertspoonfuls of the mixture, spaced slightly apart, on the baking sheet. Bake for 15–20 minutes, until slightly risen and golden brown. Remove from the oven and leave to cool on the parchment, then transfer to an airtight container. The macaroons will keep for two to three days.

Energy 65kcal/270kJ; Protein 0.7g; Carbohydrate 5.7g, of which sugars 5.7g; Fat 4.5g, of which saturates 3.9g; Cholesterol 0mg; Calcium 4mg; Fibre 0.6g; Sodium 9mg.

Meringues

These pretty meringue nests make a stunning centrepiece to the finest of tea tables. They almost look too good to eat! The crystallized petal decoration is made with raw egg white, which is unsuitable for the elderly, young and pregnant. Replace them with fresh berries, if necessary.

MAKES ABOUT 14

4 egg whites
225g/8oz/2 cups icing
   (confectioners') sugar
10ml/2 tsp vanilla extract
300ml/½ pint/1¼ cups double
   (heavy) cream

For the crystallized petals
75–100 alpine pink or violet petals
1 egg white, lightly beaten
50g/2oz/¼ cup caster (superfine)
   sugar

1 Preheat the oven to 120°C/250°F/ Gas ½. Line two baking sheets with baking parchment.

2 Whisk the egg whites until stiff. Add the icing sugar, whisking in a tablespoonful at a time, until glossy. Whisk in the vanilla extract.

3 Place large spoonfuls of meringue, spaced well apart, on the baking sheets. Make an indent in the centre. Bake for 1–1¼ hours, until the meringues are crisp. Leave to cool for a few minutes before removing the baking parchment. Place on wire racks to go cold.

4 For the crystallized petals, gather clean, dry, perfect specimens. Remove the white heels at the bases. Place beaten egg white and caster sugar in separate saucers. Paint the front and back of each petal with the egg white.

5 Dredge both sides with caster sugar. Arrange the petals on baking parchment and leave them in a warm place until completely dry. These will last for up to two days.

6 Whip the cream and spoon into the nests. Sprinkle the crystallized petals over just before serving.

Energy 178kcal/744kJ; Protein 1.5g; Carbohydrate 21.1g, of which sugars 21.1; Fat 11.5g, of which saturates 6.4 g; Cholesterol 28mg; Calcium 21.7mg; Fibre 0g; Sodium 30.8mg.

Flapjacks

The wholesome and satisfying combination of rolled oats and golden syrup makes flapjacks popular with adults and children alike. They are sweet, dense and filling, with a soft, chewy consistency. With so few ingredients, flapjacks are quick to make and guaranteed to please.

MAKES 12

175g/6oz/¾ cup unsalted butter
50g/2oz/¼ cup caster (superfine) sugar
150g/5oz/scant ⅔ cup golden (light corn) syrup
250g/9oz/1½ cups rolled oats

COOK'S TIP
Store the flapjacks in an airtight container for up to one week.

1 Preheat the oven to 180°C/350°F/ Gas 4. Grease and line a shallow 20cm/8in square baking tin (pan).

2 Place the butter, sugar and syrup in a pan and heat gently until the butter has melted.

3 Add the oats and stir until all the ingredients are combined.

4 Transfer the mixture into the tin and level the surface. Bake for 15–20 minutes, until turning golden. Leave to cool slightly, then cut into fingers and cool on a wire rack.

Energy 241kcal/1007kJ; Protein 2.7g; Carbohydrate 29.5g, of which sugars 14.3g; Fat 13.2g, of which saturates 7.2g; Cholesterol 30mg; Calcium 18mg; Fibre 1.4g; Sodium 125mg.

Luscious lemon bars

A crisp shortbread cookie base is drenched with a light and tangy lemon topping to make a sweet citrus confection. These bars make a wonderful addition to the summer tea table. Try exchanging the lemon for orange to give a new twist to this recipe.

MAKES 12

150g/5oz/1¼ cups plain
 (all-purpose) flour
90g/3½oz/7 tbsp unsalted butter,
 chilled and diced
50g/2oz/½ cup icing
 (confectioners') sugar, sifted,
 plus extra for dusting

For the topping
2 eggs
175g/6oz/scant 1 cup caster
 (superfine) sugar
finely grated rind and juice of
 1 large lemon
15ml/1 tbsp plain (all-purpose)
 flour
2.5ml/½ tsp bicarbonate of soda
 (baking soda)

1 Preheat the oven to 180°C/350°F/ Gas 4. Grease and line a 20cm/8in square shallow cake tin (pan) with baking parchment.

2 Blend the flour, butter and icing sugar in a food processor until the mixture comes together as a firm dough. Press into the base of the tin and spread smooth using the back of a spoon. Bake for 12–15 minutes.

3 To make the topping, whisk the eggs in a bowl until frothy. Add the caster sugar, a little at a time, whisking between each addition. Whisk in the lemon rind and juice, flour and bicarbonate of soda.

4 Pour over the cookie base. Bake for 20–25 minutes, until set and golden. Leave to cool slightly. Cut into bars and dust with icing sugar. Cool on a wire rack. Store in an airtight container for 2–3 days.

Energy 189kcal/795kJ; Protein 2.5g; Carbohydrate 30.3g, of which sugars 19.8g; Fat 7.3g, of which saturates 4.2g; Cholesterol 48mg; Calcium 35mg; Fibre 0.4g; Sodium 59mg.

Walnut and date bars

These wonderfully rich, moist cake bars are perfect for afternoon tea. The dates are first soaked before being added to the batter giving this sweet treat a lovely texture.

MAKES 24 BARS

225g/8oz/1⅓ cups chopped dates
250ml/8fl oz/1 cup boiling water
5ml/1 tsp bicarbonate of soda
 (baking soda)
225g/8oz/generous 1 cup caster
 (superfine) sugar

1 egg, beaten
275g/10oz/2¼ cups plain
 (all-purpose) flour
pinch of salt
75g/3oz/6 tbsp butter, softened
5ml/1 tsp vanilla extract
5ml/1 tsp baking powder
50g/2oz/½ cup chopped walnuts

1 Put the chopped dates into a warm bowl and pour the boiling water over the top; it should just cover the dates. Add the bicarbonate of soda and mix well. Leave to stand for 5–10 minutes.

2 Preheat the oven to 180°C/350°F/ Gas 4. Lightly grease a 23 x 30cm/ 9 x 12in cake tin (pan) and line with baking parchment.

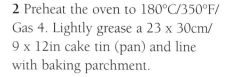

3 Combine all the remaining ingredients in a separate mixing bowl. Mix in the dates, along with the soaking water until you have a thick batter. You may find it necessary to add a little more boiling water to help the consistency.

4 Pour the batter into the tin and bake for 45 minutes until firm. Cool on a wire rack and cut into wedges.

Energy 111kcal/468kJ; Protein 2.5g; Carbohydrate 17.9g, of which sugars 10.2g; Fat 3.75g, of which saturates 0.5g; Cholesterol 0.75mg; Calcium 27mg; Fibre 1.45g; Sodium 6.8mg.

Chocolate brownies

This classic American recipe is popular with lovers of all things sweet and chocolatey. The double dose of chocolate make them rich and intense.

MAKES 15 BARS

75g/3oz dark (bittersweet)
  chocolate
115g/4oz/½ cup butter, plus extra
  for greasing
4 eggs, beaten
10ml/2 tsp vanilla extract
400g/14oz/2 cups caster (superfine)
  sugar
115g/4oz/1 cup plain (all-purpose)
  flour
25g/1oz/¼ cup unsweetened
  cocoa powder
115g/4oz dark (bittersweet)
  chocolate chips
115g/4oz/1 cup chopped walnuts

1 Preheat the oven to 190°C/375°F/ Gas 5. Liberally grease an 18 x 28cm/7 x 11in shallow baking tin (pan) and line the base with baking parchment.

2 Break the dark chocolate into pieces and put it in a heatproof bowl with the butter. Place the bowl over a pan of barely simmering water and leave until the chocolate and butter have melted. Remove from the heat and stir in the beaten eggs, vanilla and sugar. Mix all the ingredients well together.

3 Sift the flour with the cocoa powder into the chocolate mixture. Gently stir in with the chocolate chips and walnuts. Pour the mixture into the tin and level the surface.

4 Bake for about 35 minutes. To test if the brownies are fully cooked, gently shake the tin. The cakes should be set but moist. Leave to cool in the tin. Cut into squares when cold.

VARIATION
For almond brownies, add a few drops of almond extract, 75g/ 3oz/¾ cup chopped almonds and reduce the chocolate chips to 75g/3oz/½ cup.

Energy 285kcal/1190kJ; Protein 3.1g; Carbohydrate 29.6g, of which sugars 25.9g; Fat 18g, of which saturates 10.7g; Cholesterol 61mg; Calcium 37mg; Fibre 0.9g; Sodium 98mg.

Millionaire's shortbread

The combination of rich shortbread, sweet sticky caramel, and marbled milk, plain and white chocolate makes this a truly luxurious tea-time treat.

MAKES ABOUT 24

250g/9oz/2¼ cups plain
  (all-purpose) flour
75g/3oz/scant ½ cup caster
  (superfine) sugar
175g/6oz/¾ cup unsalted
  butter, softened

For the filling
90g/3½oz/7 tbsp unsalted
  butter, diced
90g/3½oz/scant ½ cup light
  muscovado (brown) sugar
2 x 400g cans sweetened
  condensed milk

For the topping
90g/3½oz plain (semisweet)
  chocolate
90g/3½oz milk chocolate
50g/2oz white chocolate

1 Preheat the oven to 180°C/350°F/ Gas 4. Lightly grease and line a 33 x 23cm/13 x 9in Swiss roll tin (jelly roll pan).

2 Put the flour and caster sugar in a bowl and rub in the butter until the mixture resembles fine breadcrumbs. Work with your hands until the mixture forms a dough.

3 Put the dough into the prepared tin and press it out with the back of a spoon to cover the base. Smooth it evenly into the tin. Prick all over with a fork and bake for about 20 minutes, or until firm to the touch and very light brown. Leave in the tin to cool.

4 To make the filling, put the butter, muscovado sugar and condensed milk into a pan and heat gently, whisking, until the sugar has dissolved.

5 Bring to the boil, stirring constantly. Reduce the heat and simmer gently, stirring constantly, for about 5–10 minutes, or until it has thickened and has turned a caramel colour. Take care that the mixture does not burn on the base of the pan. Remove from the heat.

6 Pour the caramel over the cookie base, spread evenly, then leave until cold.

7 To make the topping, melt each type of chocolate separately in heatproof bowls set over a pan of hot water. Spoon lines of plain and milk chocolate over the set caramel.

8 Add small spoonfuls of white chocolate. Use a skewer to form a marbled effect on the topping.

Energy 305kcal/1281kJ; Protein 4.6g; Carbohydrate 39.6g, of which sugars 31.6g; Fat 15.4g, of which saturates 9.6g; Cholesterol 37mg; Calcium 132mg; Fibre 0.4g; Sodium 120mg.

Cakes
and jam

Light as air, sweet Victoria sponge cake, filled with jam and cream and dusted with icing (confectioner's) sugar is the perfect finale for afternoon tea. For a truly lavish decoration add crystallized flowers to the cake top and rose petals to the buttercream in place of jam for a stunning centrepiece to the tea table. Included here too are dense and moist fruit-filled loaf cakes and nostalgic Battenberg, as well as a range of the most popular and easy-to-make fruit conserves.

Sticky gingerbread

This dark rich gingerbread cries out to be smothered in cool butter or swirls of cream cheese as a contrast to the cake's taste and texture. It tastes better when kept for a few days.

SERVES 6–8

225g/8oz/2 cups plain (all-purpose) flour
10ml/2 tsp ground ginger
5ml/1 tsp mixed (apple pie) spice
pinch of salt
2 pieces preserved stem ginger, drained and chopped
115g/4oz/½ cup butter, softened
115g/4oz/⅔ cup dark muscovado (molasses) sugar, sifted
275g/10oz/scant 1 cup black treacle (molasses)
2 eggs, beaten
2.5ml/½ tsp bicarbonate of soda (baking soda)
30ml/2 tbsp milk, warmed
butter or cream cheese, to serve

1 Preheat the oven to 160°C/325°F/ Gas 3. Lightly grease and line the base and sides of an 18cm/7in square cake tin (pan), that measures about 7.5cm/3in deep.

2 Sift the flour, ground ginger, mixed spice and salt together into a bowl. Add the stem ginger and toss it in the flour to coat thoroughly.

3 In a separate bowl, cream the butter and sugar together until fluffy, then gradually beat in the treacle. Gradually beat in the eggs, then the flour mixture.

4 Dissolve the bicarbonate of soda in the milk and gradually beat into the batter. Pour into the prepared tin and bake for 45 minutes. Reduce the oven temperature to 150°C/300°F/ Gas 2 and bake for a further 30 minutes. To test whether the cake is cooked, insert a metal skewer into the middle: it should come out clean.

5 Cool for 5 minutes in the tin and then turn out on to a wire rack to cool completely. Keep for two to three days in an airtight container so that the gingerbread becomes sticky and moist. Cut into pieces and serve with butter or cream cheese.

Energy 373kcal/1572kJ; Protein 5.2g; Carbohydrate 60.9g, of which sugars 38.7g; Fat 13.9g, of which saturates 8.1g; Cholesterol 78.5mg; Calcium 253.6mg; Fibre 0.9g; Sodium 170.5mg.

Banana bread

This wholesome banana bread is not overly sweet. It makes a filling and nutritious addition to the tea table. Serve it alone or with jam or marmalade.

SERVES 10

115g/4oz/½ cup butter, plus extra
   for greasing
5ml/1 tsp bicarbonate of soda
   (baking soda)
225g/8oz/2 cups wholemeal
   (whole-wheat) flour
2 eggs, beaten
3 very ripe bananas
30–45ml/2–3 tbsp unsweetened
   coconut milk or soya milk

1 Preheat the oven to 180°C/350°F/ Gas 4. Grease and line the base of a 23 x 13cm/9 x 5in loaf tin.

2 Cream the butter in a bowl until it is light and fluffy. Sift the bicarbonate of soda with the flour, then add to the butter, alternating with the eggs.

COOK'S TIPS
• Use really ripe bananas for this recipe to give a full, sweet fruity flavour. They will also be easier to mash to a smooth consistency.
• Do not peel the bananas until ready to use them or they will discolour.

3 Peel the bananas and slice them into a bowl. Mash them thoroughly using a fork. Mix in the coconut milk or soya milk, then stir into the cake mixture.

4 Spoon the mixture into the loaf tin and level the top with a spoon. Bake for about 1¼ hours or until a fine skewer inserted in the centre comes out clean. Cool on a wire rack.

Energy 226kcal/955kJ; Protein 5.2g; Carbohydrate 37.2g, of which sugars 19.6g; Fat 7.4g, of which saturates 3.8g; Cholesterol 51.9mg; Calcium 46.1mg; Fibre 1.9g; Sodium 55.3mg.

Battenberg

Immediately identifiable, Battenberg cake has a characteristic light sponge that is set in a chequerboard arrangement of pink and yellow cake. It is encased in a smooth cover of marzipan and served in dainty slices. Delicious!

SERVES 14

175g/6oz/¾ cup butter, softened
175g/6oz/scant 1 cup caster
  (superfine) sugar
3 large (US extra large) eggs,
  lightly beaten
175g/6oz/1½ cups self-raising
  (self-rising) flour, sifted
pinch of salt
2.5ml/½ tsp red food colouring
2.5ml/½ tsp rosewater
2.5ml/½ tsp orange flower water,
  or almond extract
450g/1lb marzipan
90ml/6 tbsp apricot jam
30ml/2 tbsp sugar

1 Preheat the oven to 190°C/375°F/ Gas 5. Lightly grease a Swiss roll tin (jelly roll pan), 30 x 20 x 2.5cm (12 x 8 x 1in). Lightly grease the base and line it with baking parchment.

2 Cut a strip of cardboard to fit the inside of the tin. Cover with foil, lightly grease and wedge in place. In a large bowl, beat the butter with the caster sugar until creamy. Add the eggs and beat well. Lightly fold in the flour and salt.

3 Put half the mixture in a clean bowl and mix in the red food colouring and rosewater until evenly tinted. Turn into one side of the tin.

4 Mix the orange flower water or almond extract into the remaining batter and turn into the empty side of the tin. Smooth into the corners.

5 Bake for 20 minutes until risen and firm to the touch. Leave to stand for 5 minutes. Slide the blade of a knife between cake, tin and foil strip, and turn out on to a wire rack lined with silicone paper. Remove the lining paper. Leave to go cold.

6 Trim the cake so that each half measures 28 x 9cm (11 x 3½in). Cut each slab in half lengthways so there are four equal pieces.

7 In a pan, bring the jam and sugar slowly to the boil, stirring constantly. Boil for 30–60 seconds. Remove from the heat.

8 To assemble the cake, brush the top of each plain cake strip with the syrup and press a pink strip on top. Brush one side of each cake stack with syrup and press them together to make a chequerboard pattern.

9 Roll out the marzipan to 28cm/ 11in square. Brush the cake top with syrup, and place the cake syrup-side down 1cm/½in from one edge of the marzipan. Brush the rest of the cake with syrup. Wrap the marzipan over and around the cake, smoothing it firmly with your hand. Press firmly at the join to seal. Trim away any excess marzipan.

Energy 355kcal/1492kJ; Protein 4.4g; Carbohydrate 51.2g, of which sugars 41.7g; Fat 15.7g, of which saturates 7.5g; Cholesterol 70mg; Calcium 55mg; Fibre 1g; Sodium 117mg.

Chocolate chip walnut cake

The tangy flavour of orange works well in this chocolate and nut loaf. It can be finished simply with a generous dusting of icing sugar, or as here with a zesty orange topping.

SERVES 6–8

115g/4oz/1 cup plain (all-purpose) flour
25g/1oz/¼ cup cornflour (cornstarch)
5ml/1 tsp baking powder
115g/4oz/½ cup butter, at room temperature
115g/4oz/½ cup golden caster (superfine) sugar
2 eggs, lightly beaten
75g/3oz/½ cup plain (semisweet), milk or white chocolate chips
50g/2oz/½ cup chopped walnuts
finely grated rind of ½ orange

For the topping
115g/4oz/1 cup icing (confectioners') sugar, sifted, plus extra for dusting
20–30ml/4 tsp–2 tbsp freshly squeezed orange juice
walnut halves, to decorate

1 Preheat the oven to 180°C/350°F/ Gas 4. Lightly grease and line a 450g/1lb loaf tin (pan) with baking parchment.

2 In a bowl, sift the flour, cornflour and baking powder together twice, so that the dry ingredients are well mixed and set aside.

3 In a large mixing bowl, beat the butter and caster sugar until light and fluffy. Add the eggs a little at a time, beating well after each addition. If the mixture curdles, beat in 15ml/1 tbsp of the flour mixture after each egg.

4 Gently fold half of the sifted flour into the creamed mixture.

5 Add the chocolate chips, walnuts and orange rind, then the rest of the flour. Fold in until just blended, taking care not to overmix.

6 Spoon the mixture into the prepared loaf tin and smooth the top level. Bake for 55 minutes in the preheated oven or until firm and a warmed skewer inserted into the centre comes out clean. Leave to stand in the tin for 5 minutes then turn out to cool on a wire rack.

7 To decorate the cake, place the icing sugar in a bowl. Stir in the orange juice until it is the consistency of thick cream. Drizzle over the cake, then decorate with walnut halves dusted with icing sugar. Leave to set before serving. Store in an airtight container.

Energy 470kcal/1956kJ; Protein 7.5g; Carbohydrate 36g, of which sugars 19g; Fat 33.6g, of which saturates 9.6g; Cholesterol 78mg; Calcium 67.8mg; Fibre 1.6g; Sodium 114mg.

Chocolate cake

A rich luxurious chocolate cake is a staple of every self-respecting tea table. The intense taste and aroma of chocolate make it a feast for the senses.

SERVES 8

225g/8oz/2 cups plain (all-purpose) flour
5ml/1 tsp bicarbonate of soda (baking soda)
50g/2oz/½ cup unsweetened cocoa powder
125g/4½oz/9 tbsp butter, softened
250g/9oz/1¼ cups caster (superfine) sugar
3 eggs, beaten
250ml/8fl oz/1 cup buttermilk

For the buttercream
175g/6oz/1½ cups icing (confectioners') sugar
115g/4oz/½ cup unsalted butter, softened
few drops of vanilla extract
50g/2oz dark (bittersweet) chocolate

1 Preheat the oven to 180°C/350°F/ Gas 4. Grease two 20cm/8in cake tins (pans) and line the bases with baking parchment. Sift the flour with the bicarbonate of soda and cocoa.

2 In another bowl, beat the butter and sugar until light and fluffy. Gradually beat in the eggs, then beat in the flour and buttermilk.

3 Spoon into the prepared tins. Place into the hot oven and cook for 30–35 minutes until firm to the touch. Turn out of the tins, peel off the paper and leave on a wire rack to cool completely.

4 To make the chocolate buttercream, sift the icing sugar into a bowl. In a separate bowl, beat the butter until very soft and creamy. Beat in half the sifted icing sugar until smooth and light. Gradually beat in the remaining sugar and the vanilla extract.

5 Break the chocolate into squares and put in a heatproof bowl set over a pan of gently simmering water until melted. Mix the chocolate into the buttercream. Use half to sandwich the cakes together, and spread the rest over the top.

Energy 430kcal/1790kJ; Protein 7.8g; Carbohydrate 29.5g, of which sugars 28.8g; Fat 32.1g, of which saturates 13.6g; Cholesterol 96mg; Calcium 92mg; Fibre 1.9g; Sodium 125mg.

Courgette and double-ginger cake

Both fresh and preserved ginger are used to flavour this unusual tea bread. It is delicious served warm, cut into thick slices and spread with butter.

SERVES 8–10

3 eggs
225g/8oz/generous 1 cup caster
  (superfine) sugar
250ml/8fl oz/1 cup sunflower oil
5ml/1 tsp vanilla extract
15ml/1 tbsp syrup from a jar of
  preserved stem ginger
225g/8oz/1⅓ cups courgettes
  (zucchini), grated
2.5cm/1in piece fresh root
  ginger, grated
350g/12oz/3 cups plain
  (all-purpose) flour
5ml/1 tsp baking powder
pinch of salt
5ml/1 tsp ground cinnamon
2 pieces preserved stem ginger,
  chopped
15ml/1 tbsp demerara (raw) sugar

1 Preheat the oven to 190°C/325°F/ Gas 5. Lightly grease and line a 900g/2lb loaf tin (pan).

2 In a mixing bowl, using an electric beater or wooden spoon, beat together the eggs and sugar until light and increased in volume. Continue to beat while adding the oil in a steady trickle until a batter forms.

3 Mix in the vanilla extract and ginger syrup, then stir in the courgettes and fresh ginger.

4 Sift together the flour, baking powder, salt and cinnamon into the batter in batches and beat well to combine after each addition.

5 Fill the prepared tin with the batter. then sprinkle over the chopped ginger and demerara sugar.

6 Bake for 1 hour, until a skewer inserted into the centre comes out clean. Leave to cool for 20 minutes, then turn out on to a wire rack.

Energy 252kcal/1060kJ; Protein 5.6g; Carbohydrate 35.6g, of which sugars 8.8g; Fat 10.7g, of which saturates 1.6g; Cholesterol 57mg; Calcium 73mg; Fibre 1.3g; Sodium 82mg.

Madeira cake

This sugar-crusted cake is soaked in lemon syrup, so it is infused with tangy citrus flavour and stays moist. It is wonderful with a cup of lemon tea, or a fruit-flavoured herbal blend.

SERVES 10

250g/9oz/1 cup plus 2 tbsp butter, softened
225g/8oz/generous 1 cup caster (superfine) sugar
5 eggs
275g/10oz/2½ cups plain (all-purpose) flour
10ml/2 tsp baking powder
pinch of salt

For the sugar crust
60ml/4 tbsp lemon juice
15ml/1 tbsp golden (light corn) syrup
30ml/2 tbsp sugar

1 Preheat the oven to 180°C/350°F/ Gas 4. Grease a 900g/2lb loaf tin (pan) with butter.

2 Beat the butter and sugar until light and creamy, then gradually beat in the eggs until you have a smooth consistency.

3 Sift over the flour, baking powder and salt, and fold in gently. Spoon into the prepared tin, level the top and bake for 1¼ hours, until a skewer pushed into the centre comes out clean.

4 Remove the cake from the oven and, while still warm and in the tin, use a skewer to pierce it several times right the way through. Warm the lemon juice and syrup together, add the sugar and immediately spoon over the cake so the flavoured syrup soaks through but leaves some sugar crystals on the top. Chill the cake for several hours or overnight.

Energy 422kcal/1764kJ; Protein 6g; Carbohydrate 49.4g, of which sugars 28.4g; Fat 23.7g, of which saturates 13.9g; Cholesterol 148mg; Calcium 71mg; Fibre 0.9g; Sodium 193mg.

Iced Victoria sponge

Crystallized roses grace this splendid Victoria sandwich. Filled with rose-scented buttercream, it makes a breath-taking centrepiece. You could use jam and buttercream to sandwich the layers.

SERVES 10–12

225g/8oz/1 cup butter, softened
225g/8oz/generous 1 cup caster
  (superfine) sugar
4 eggs
225g/8oz/2 cups self-raising
  (self-rising) flour
5ml/1 tsp baking powder

For the filling
115g/4oz/½ cup butter, softened
115g/4oz/1 cup icing
  (confectioners') sugar
60ml/4 tbsp sweetly scented
  rose petals

For the topping
225g/8oz/2 cups icing
  (confectioners') sugar
30–45ml/2–3tbsp rose water
crystallized roses and rose petals

1 Preheat the oven to 180°C/350°F/ Gas 4. Lightly grease and line two 20cm/8in round sandwich tins (layer pans).

2 Beat the butter with the caster sugar until light and fluffy. Add the eggs one at a time, beating well after each. Sift over the flour and baking powder together, and beat well.

3 Divide the mixture between the two sandwich tins and bake for 25 minutes until firm to the touch. Transfer to a wire rack to cool.

4 To make the filling, beat the softened butter until light and creamy. Add the icing sugar until all has been incorporated.

5 Chop the rose petals finely and add to the butter mixture. Spread between the two halves of the cooled cake.

6 To make the topping, beat the icing sugar in a bowl with 30ml/ 2 tbsp of the rose water to give a consistency that thickly coats the back of a spoon. Add more rose water, drop by drop, if necessary.

7 Spoon the icing over the cake, allowing it to run down the sides. Decorate with a circle of crystallized roses and petals.

CAUTION
Raw eggs should not be consumed by pregnant women, the young and elderly.

CRYSTALLIZED ROSES

1 egg white, or reconstituted
  powdered egg white
50g/2oz/¼ cup caster
  (superfine) sugar
6–8 pink roses, and several
  rose petals

1 Gather your flowers and petals when dry. Remove the white heel at the base of any individual petals as it tastes bitter.

2 Lightly beat the egg white and place in a saucer. Put the caster sugar in a separate saucer.

3 Using an artist's brush, paint the flowerhead, or petals front and back, with egg white.

4 Dredge with caster sugar until all are well coated.

5 Lay individual petals and flowers on sheets of baking parchment and keep them in a warm, dry place overnight, or until crisp. Store in a sealed container for up to 2 days.

Energy 557kcal/2339kJ; Protein 4.3g; Carbohydrate 83.4g, of which sugars 69.1g; Fat 25.2g, of which saturates 15.9g; Cholesterol 129mg; Calcium 75mg; Fibre 0.6g; Sodium 240mg.

Summer strawberry roulade

The essential English summer fruit, strawberries make a welcome appearance to any afternoon tea setting. This delicate roulade is light and moreish.

SERVES 8

3 eggs
115g/4oz/½ cup caster (superfine) sugar, plus extra for dusting
115g/4oz/1 cup plain (all-purpose) flour
150g/5oz/½ cup Greek (US strained plain) yogurt
150g/5oz/½ cup plain fromage frais
225g/8oz/2 cups strawberries, sliced
strawberries, to decorate

1 Preheat the oven to 200°C/400°F/Gas 6. Lightly grease and line a 33 x 23cm/13 x 9in Swiss roll tin (jelly roll pan).

2 Mix together the Greek yogurt and fromage frais.

3 Place the eggs and sugar in a large bowl over a pan of simmering water. Whisk, using an electric hand whisk, until the mixture is pale, creamy and thick enough to leave a trail on the surface.

4 Remove the bowl from the heat and whisk the mixture until cool.

5 Sift half the flour into the sugar mixture. Fold in gently with a metal spoon. Sift in the rest of the flour. Fold in with 15ml/1 tbsp hot water.

6 Pour the mixture into the prepared tin, tilting the tin to level the surface. Bake for 10–15 minutes or until well-risen, golden brown and firm to the touch.

7 Sprinkle a sheet of non-stick baking paper with the remaining caster sugar.

8 Turn out the hot cake on to the paper, trim the edges and roll up the cake. Place seam-side down on a wire rack and allow to go cold, then carefully unroll the cake. Spread with yogurt mixture. Scatter the strawberries on top. Re-roll the cake and serve immediately

Energy 271kcal/1127kJ; Protein 4.7g; Carbohydrate 16.7g, of which sugars 11.9g; Fat 21.1g, of which saturates 11.2g; Cholesterol 114mg; Calcium 56mg; Fibre 1.2g; Sodium 35mg.

Dundee cake

A classic fruit cake, made with mixed peel, dried fruit, almonds and spices. The cake surface is covered with decreasing circles of whole blanched almonds.

SERVES 16–20

175g/6oz/¾ cup butter
175g/6oz/¾ cup soft light
  brown sugar
3 eggs
225g/8oz/2 cups plain
  (all-purpose) flour
10ml/2 tsp baking powder
5ml/1 tsp ground cinnamon
pinch of ground cloves
pinch of grated nutmeg
225g/8oz/generous 1½ cups
  sultanas (golden raisins)
175g/6oz/¾ cup glacé
  (candied) cherries
115g/4oz/⅔ cup mixed
  chopped peel
50g/2oz/½ cup blanched almonds,
  roughly chopped
grated rind of 1 lemon
30ml/2 tbsp brandy
75g/3oz/¾ cup whole blanched
  almonds, to decorate

1 Preheat the oven to 160°C/325°F/Gas 3. Lightly grease and line a 20cm/8in round, deep cake tin (pan).

2 Cream the butter and sugar together in a large mixing bowl. Add the eggs, one at a time, beating thoroughly after each addition.

COOK'S TIP
All rich fruit cakes improve in flavour if left in a cool place for up to 3 months. Wrap the cake in baking parchment and a double layer of foil.

3 Sift the flour, baking powder and spices together. Fold into the creamed mixture alternately with the remaining ingredients, apart from the whole almonds. Mix until evenly blended. Transfer the mixture to the prepared tin and smooth the surface, making a dip in the centre.

4 Decorate the top by pressing the almonds in decreasing circles over the entire surface.

5 Bake for 2–2¼ hours, until a skewer inserted in the centre comes out clean. Allow to cool slightly then turn out on to a wire rack to go cold.

Energy 321kcal/1347kJ; Protein 4.7g; Carbohydrate 44.2g, of which sugars 33.3g; Fat 14.7g, of which saturates 6.4g; Cholesterol 59mg; Calcium 76mg; Fibre 1.7g; Sodium 107mg.

Fruit jams and jellies

There's nothing to compare with homemade jam, bursting with fruit, spread thickly over a slice of buttered bread or a delicious warm scone at tea time. Here are six of the most popular recipes, make them when you have a glut of fruit in the summer months.

Strawberry jam

Perfectly ripe strawberries, shiny and deep red in colour, are the main ingredient of this most popular jam.

MAKES ABOUT 1.4KG/3LB

1kg/2¼lb/8 cups strawberries, hulled
900g/2lb/4 cups sugar
juice of 2 lemons

1 Layer the hulled strawberries with the sugar in a large bowl. Cover with clear film (plastic wrap) and leave overnight.

2 Put the strawberries into a large heavy pan. Add the lemon juice. Gradually bring to the boil, over a low heat, stirring until the sugar has dissolved.

3 Boil steadily for 10–15 minutes, or until the jam reaches setting point (*see box below*). When it is ready, cool for 10 minutes in the pan.

4 Pour into warm sterilized jars, filling them right to the top. Cover and seal while the jam is still hot and label when the jars are cold.

5 Store in a cool dark place for up to one year.

SETTING POINT
The point at which jam sets is 105°C/220°F. If you don't have a sugar thermometer, put 10ml/ 2 tsp of the jam on to a chilled saucer. Chill for 3 minutes, then push the jam gently with your finger; if wrinkles form it is ready. If not, continue boiling, but keep checking regularly.

Energy 3816kcal/16259kJ; Protein 12.5g; Carbohydrate 1000.5g, of which sugars 1000.5g; Fat 1g, of which saturates 0g; Cholesterol 0mg; Calcium 637mg; Fibre 11g; Sodium 114mg.

Raspberry jam

For many, this is the best of all jams; it is delicious with scones and cream. Raspberries are low in pectin and acid, so they will not set firmly, but a soft set is perfect for this jam.

MAKES ABOUT 3.1KG/7LB

1.8kg/4lb/10⅔ cups firm raspberries
juice of 1 large lemon
1.8kg/4lb/9 cups preserving sugar, warmed

1 Put 175g/6oz/1 cup of the raspberries into a large, heavy pan and crush them. Add the rest of the fruit and the lemon juice. Bring to the boil, simmer until soft and pulpy.

2 Add the sugar and stir until dissolved, then bring back to the boil and boil rapidly until setting point is reached.

3 Pour the jam into warmed sterilized jars, filling to the top. Cover and seal the jars. Label when cold, and store in a cold, dark place for up to 6 months.

Energy 7542kcal/32220kJ; Protein 34.2g; Carbohydrate 1963.8g, of which sugars 1963.8g; Fat 5.4g, of which saturates 1.8g; Cholesterol 0mg; Calcium 1.4mg; Fibre 45g; Sodium 162mg.

Bramble jelly

This jelly has an excellent intense, fruity flavour. Make sure you include a few red unripe berries in the pan for a good fruit set.

MAKES ABOUT 900G/2LB

900g/2lb/8 cups blackberries
juice of 1 lemon
about 900g/2lb/4 cups caster (superfine) sugar

1 Put the fruit, 300ml/½ pint/1¼ cups water and the lemon juice in a large, heavy pan. Cover and cook for 15–30 minutes or until the blackberries are very soft.

2 Ladle into a jelly bag, set over a large bowl. Leave to strain overnight. Discard the fruit pulp. Measure the juice and add 450g/1lb/ 2 cups sugar to every 600ml/1 pint/2½ cups juice.

3 Place the sugar and liquid in a large, heavy pan and bring slowly to the boil, stirring all the time. When setting point is reached (see page 92), skim off any scum and pour into warm sterilized jars. Cover and seal while the jelly is still hot. Label when the jars are cold. Store for up to 6 months in a cool, dry place.

Energy 3771kcal/16065kJ; Protein 12.6g; Carbohydrate 986.4g, of which sugars 986.4g; Fat 1.8g, of which saturates 0g; Cholesterol 0mg; Calcium 846mg; Fibre 27.9g; Sodium 72mg.

Apricot conserve

If you miss the short apricot season, you can enjoy the taste of sweet, tangy apricot jam all year round.

MAKES ABOUT 2KG/4½LB

675g/1½lb dried apricots, soaked overnight in 900ml/
  1½ pints/3¾ cups apple juice
juice and grated rind of 2 unwaxed lemons
675g/1½lb/scant 3½ cups preserving sugar
50g/2oz/½ cup blanched almonds, coarsely chopped

1 Pour the soaked apricots and juice into a preserving pan and add the lemon juice and rind. Bring to the boil, then lower the heat and simmer for 15–20 minutes until soft.

2 Add the sugar to the pan and bring to the boil, stirring until the sugar has completely dissolved. Boil for 15–20 minutes, or until setting point is reached.

3 Stir the chopped almonds into the jam and leave to stand for about 15 minutes, then pour the jam into warmed, sterilized jars. Seal, then leave to cool. Label and store in a cool, dark place for up to one year.

Energy 4032kcal/17163kJ; Protein 40.9g; Carbohydrate 955.2g, of which sugars 953.8g; Fat 31.9g, of which saturates 2.2g; Cholesterol 0mg; Calcium 970mg; Fibre 46.2g; Sodium 142mg.

Damson jam

Dark, plump damsons are now commercially available. They produce a deeply coloured and richly flavoured jam.

MAKES ABOUT 4KG/4½LB

1kg/2¼lb damsons or wild plums
1.4litres/2¼ pints/6 cups water
1 kg/2¼lb/5 cups preserving sugar

1 Put the damsons in a preserving pan and pour in the water. Bring to the boil, then reduce the heat and simmer gently until the damsons are soft. Add the sugar and stir.

2 Bring the mixture to the boil. Skim off the stones (pits) as they rise to the surface. Boil to setting point. Remove from the heat and leave to cool for 10 minutes.

3 Pour into warmed sterilized jars, cover and seal. Allow to cool, then label. Store in a cool, dark place for 1 year.

Energy 4320kcal/18430kJ; Protein 10g; Carbohydrate 1141g, of which sugars 1141g; Fat 0g, of which saturates 0g; Cholesterol 0mg; Calcium 770mg; Fibre 18g; Sodium 80mg.

Lemon curd

This classic tangy, creamy curd is enduringly popular. It is delicious spread thickly over freshly baked white bread, or used to fill homemade tarts, or as a filling for Victoria sandwich cakes.

MAKES ABOUT 450G/1LB

3 unwaxed lemons
200g/7oz/1 cup caster (superfine)
  sugar
115g/4oz/8 tbsp unsalted
  butter, diced
2 large (US extra large) eggs and
  2 large egg yolks

4 Stir the mixture constantly over the heat until the lemon curd thickens and lightly coats the back of a wooden spoon.

5 Remove the pan from the heat and pour the curd into small, warmed sterilized jars. Cover and seal immediately. Allow to cool and label. Store in a cool, dark place, ideally in the refrigerator. Use within 3 months. Once opened, it is essential to store the lemon curd in the refrigerator and use quickly.

VARIATION
Use oranges to make orange curd.

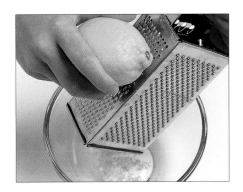

1 Wash the lemons, then grate the rind into a large heatproof bowl. Squeeze the juice into the bowl.

2 Set the bowl over a pan of gently simmering water and add the sugar and butter. Stir until the sugar has dissolved and the butter melted.

3 Put the eggs and yolks in a bowl and beat together. Pour the eggs through a sieve (strainer) into the lemon mixture, and whisk well.

Energy 1927kcal/8056kJ; Protein 20.7g; Carbohydrate 212.1g, of which sugars 212.1g; Fat 116.8g, of which saturates 66.2g; Cholesterol 1029mg; Calcium 294mg; Fibre 0g; Sodium 871mg.

Index